1

Forgotten Veterans

Patrick - thanks for support of the The troops.
Steve

Stephen M. Reay

 Requests for such permission or further information should be addressed to S & J Publishing, 558 Shoshone St., Grand Junction, CO 81504, USA.
Phone: 970-523-0292
E-Mail: reayk@msn.com

Additional Copies of this publication can be purchased at www.amazon.com.

ISBN 978-1-60643-404-8

Printed in the United States of America.

Dedication

To my best friend for 37 years, my wife Kay, who put endless hours of work into *The Forgotten Veterans*. Her years as a special education teacher and her spiritual values helped inspire this effort. And to my adventurous children, Darrin, Whose passion is climbing 14,000 ft. mountains wherever he can find them, and Allison, the professional sky diving videographer. Their enthusiasm for life continues to motivate me to new experiences.

MANY THANKS

I would like to take this opportunity to thank the many friends and family who have had a hand in bringing this book to fruition. First, I want to express my appreciation to my brother, Jim, for his loyalty and amazing insight. Many thanks to my co-workers: recreation therapists, Howard Fedden and Laurie Morris, who put up with me for too many years. Thanks also to Sandy Hockett, who's creative illustrations were invaluable. The wit and knowledge of Joni Lyons, VA ambulatory care nurse, was very helpful as was Stephanie Bomar, whose organizational skills and terrific sense of humor were always an inspiration. My long time friend, Kent Thompson, Ph.D., helped launch the writing of this book.

Table of Contents

Introduction

General Sherman said, "War is Hell!" Coming home from war can be a "Hell" of another kind. The *Forgotten Veterans* is a story of what sometimes happens to returning combat veterans who are wounded physically or psychologically in military service. It's a part of the aftermath of war that most of us are fortunate to never experience. Today, as the cloud of war continues over America, this story of the long-term effects of combat on the lives of thousands of servicemen and women is more compelling than ever. This is not an expose or a call to arms, but rather a personal perspective on a vital, but scarcely touched part of the story of some of those who sacrificed much in defense of the nation.

The Forgotten Veterans is a personal account over a 30 year period of a recreation therapist at a veterans' hospital in a small western town. It is an anthology of stories focusing on the hope, comedy, personal courage and sometimes tragedy of returning veterans who for many reasons, some physical and some psychological, cannot assimilate into their own families and communities. These men and women live an "institutionalized" existence through no fault of their own. It is the worst case of being at the wrong place at the wrong time. Some have simply "slipped through the cracks" of society. In nearly every case, the patients in veterans' hospitals ask little in return but comfort for their wounds and a place to find hope and solace. The stories in the book are true. In some cases, they are composites of different people and times, but in every case, the described words and actions really occurred. In all cases the actual names have been changed to protect the privacy of individuals.

The poignant story of these *Forgotten Veterans* is told by the principal character, Scott Reemers, a Vietnam veteran himself, who has a first-hand understanding of the horrors of combat and the challenges faced by young men and women trying to return to their civilian lives, jobs and families. Often, these veterans have no refuge other than the hospital and many will spend the rest of their days isolated from the life they once knew. Scott and his fellow therapists spend their careers trying to make the daily lives of the veteran patients as bearable as possible. Each patient makes a new, unforgettable impression on the hospital staff. No one reading these stories can help but be touched by the plight of these warriors who stood tall in defending their country and who, in their time of need, have frequently been pushed from the Nation's attention.

The Forgotten Veterans is a chronology of real events, simple by themselves, but put together in context by one who experienced veterans' problems first hand. This book provides a meaningful and timely testimony to the need to preserve America's commitment to all of its veterans, particularly those whose lives have been wounded forever.

Chapter 1

In early evening, the February snow fell softly to the ground outside the 100 year old red brick buildings of the Sheridan, Wyoming, Veterans Administration (VA) Hospital. Sunlight refracted off the frozen snow outside the hospital, a hard glimmer of pearly white sheen that hurt his eyes, but he didn't care—the sting made him feel alive. The tingle made him take notice. Recreational therapist, Scott Reemers, was driving home for a late dinner with his wife, Kate, a special education school teacher. He knew she would be worried because of the blizzards that can come up quickly and deadly. Scott, thinking of his day's "work," smiled to himself that here he was, actually getting paid, to help "his boys"--fellow military veterans--regain their sense of self and community by playing games, watching movies, socializing with each other and in some cases just feeling safe from the outside world. Even after many years "on the job" he still liked going to work, discussing the day's events with his co-workers, and interacting with his patients. Just today, he had mentioned to Hank Farrow, a fellow recreational therapist, how much he enjoyed the interaction with this strange bunch of characters. Scott and Hank had become close friends and often shared their experiences both at work and with their families.

The calm of the evening reflected the sense of gratitude and fulfillment Scott felt his job brought to him. He counted himself among the lucky ones who actually enjoyed going to work each day. He had told Kate this morning he might be home late and she knew what that meant.

At that very moment, however, all was not calm in Unit 64, the psychiatric section where Scott had been working only 30 minutes before. Violence didn't happen often in the Sheridan hospital, but when it did, it came full force. On this particular evening, Betty Smith, a psychiatric nurse, well qualified and experienced, made a terrible mistake. Betty had been having problems at home and was distracted by that morning's fight with her husband. This proved fatal. While on duty in the closed psychiatric unit she went into the room of a patient alone. God only knows what demons haunted this veteran, but he snapped, brutally beating her to death with his bare hands. A second patient, Joe Davis, made a courageous effort to stop the attack but was unsuccessful. He had heard the screams and tried to rescue Betty. Joe's efforts were too late. Ironically, Betty had only two weeks left before she planned to retire and get away from the dangers of the unit.

Scott, along with the other hospital staff members, would not only grieve the loss of their co-worker but remember their own personal encounters with human violence. In 1970, fourteen years before Betty's death, Scott Reemers was an E-3, private first class, U. S. Army soldier, sitting atop another hill overlooking another village, only this time there wasn't even the hint of snow. He was in a country called Vietnam. Although born in Ohio in 1945, six months before the dropping of the atomic bombs on Hiroshima and Nagasaki, Scott grew up in southern Colorado's San Luis Valley in Monte Vista, a small town of 4,600, 112 miles southwest of Colorado Springs. In fact, Scott was a fixture on the local high school's football and baseball teams from 1960 until his graduation in 1963. Sports gave him a direction, an identity, and an appreciation of team spirit. Like other Americans for many generations, it would be difficult to picture life without a competitive athletic involvement and participation. That deep-seated, almost soulful linkage to sports would later be the driving force that Scott would take to work daily during his 30 year stint at the Sheridan VA Hospital. Scott had been the starting quarterback on his team. This experience gave him an insight to leadership that served him well. Scott realized that his job at the VA hospital brought him as close as he could ever hope to a career in sports.

After graduation in 1963, Scott enrolled in Adams State College in nearby Alamosa, Colorado, with a football scholarship – partly to get an education and partly because his friends were doing the same. At first, Scott dreamed of a career as a professional player, but he soon realized that moving to that level of play just wasn't in the cards. His enthusiasm for school soon dissipated. For several years, his major motive to stay in school was to avoid being drafted into the Army. He even took a few months off and went to California seeking something different. He soon found that working as a gas station attendant in Los Angeles wasn't anything like what he might want. One night, a drunken robber with a knife and bad intentions convinced Scott life in California just wasn't for him. After that, he returned to Adams State with a renewed sense of dedication. It was during that time that hostilities were escalating in a far off part of the world about which few Americans knew anything. All Scott knew was that he didn't want to go there. He went to enough classes and passed enough tests at Adams State so that in May of 1969 he graduated with a bachelor's degree in recreation. He immediately received a draft lottery number of 189, meaning he definitely would be called within two months and would, like 95% of all draftees at that time, end up in Southeast Asia. Scott often remembered how as college graduation drew closer, he realized that he had used up his college deferment and would probably be drafted the moment he had his degree. Scott and four or five high school buddies decided to enlist rather than wait to be drafted. They had heard that enlisting might give them a chance to avoid being sent to Vietnam. In a decision motivated totally by a desire to spend the least amount of time possible in the Army, he enlisted in June of 1969.

When Scott and his friends reported to the induction center they started to realize this was going to be serious business. Scott's friend, Frank, was particularly worried. When they arrived in Denver for their physical exams, they saw a huge, mean looking marine sergeant approaching. He was looking the recruits up and down and then much to the surprise and dismay of Scott's friend, he chose Frank to be mustered into the Marines rather than the Army. Their first thought went to their friend Ralph, the starting fullback on the high school football team. He had joined the Marines and was killed in Vietnam in 1965. As fate would have it, Frank spent his two years in the Marines at the stateside base near El Toro, California. Unlike Scott, he never even saw Vietnam. Years later, they joked about Frank's good luck. Scott was sent to Ft. Sill, Oklahoma, to be trained as a "fire direction controller." He was the guy who told the artillery personnel where to shoot. After twelve weeks of grueling boot camp, combat and artillery training, Scott and the rest of the Americal Company were informed that they would be going to Vietnam. None of them really knew why.

In 1965, President Lyndon Johnson had approved intense bombing of North Vietnam and the dispatch of a large force of United States combat troops into South Vietnam in order to prevent the further infiltration of communism into that part of the world. This sounded like political mumbo-jumbo to Scott and his fellow recruits. Each evening in the barracks, they spent hours wondering when their time would come to ship out. Finally, the day came. They all knew that they were headed to a country that they knew little about and for reasons that they understood even less. Scott did know how difficult it would be to say good-bye to his fiancé, family and friends.

Scott's flight had a short, re-fueling stop in Anchorage, Alaska. When he deplaned for a quick rest break, the temperature was 50 degrees below zero which did nothing to lift his spirits. Scott and his friends decided that they couldn't wait to get to Vietnam. Even though they might be getting shot at, at least it would be warm. Despite the cold, Scott knew his life was going to change in combat and maybe not for the better. He wasn't afraid exactly, but was just anxious to see what the war was all about and of course, to get it over as quickly as possible. After reboarding, he noticed how somber the mood had become. Scott was twenty-five at the time and one of the oldest men on the plane. Most of them weren't even men. As he glanced from face to face, he saw boys who had probably been playing high school sports just six months earlier. The soldier on his left was from Madison, Wisconsin. Ron had also played quarterback for his high school football team. Ron had recently become a Christian and spoke about his relationship with God. Scott was most likely one of many who gave their hearts to God on that flight. There was very little laughter or joy on the plane. As they neared their destination of Cam Ranh Bay, South Vietnam, they could see the rolling waves of the ocean.

The South China Sea is a beautiful blue body of water located on the eastern coast of South Vietnam. But, the beauty of that sea couldn't overcome the feeling of dread that seemed to envelop everyone as they departed from the plane. Before landing, the first sergeant had warned everyone about the hazards of the rough currents in the sea. Scott never forgot his command, "Do not swim in the South China Sea." He recalled later how that sea took the lives of several American soldiers that first day. Within 24 hours of landing, five members of his company, totally ignoring the orders to stay out of the rough water, had drowned. Scott did not think that was a good sign. He thought of their families back home. He wondered just how the Army would explain their deaths.

Turned out there were plenty of excuses to go around covering meaningless loss of life. Many of these young boys had never seen the ocean before and had no idea of how dangerous ocean currents could be, especially in these waters. And boys being boys, the first thing that several of them did was to go swimming. Five soldiers drowned that first day. Others watched in horror as these young men, who had become friends, were washed away in the South China Sea.

Scott was bombarded with memories from the summer of 1960. It had been a perfect summer day in southern Colorado. Scott and 5 of his friends decided to go rafting in the lake at the Soldiers and Sailors Home near Monte Vista. The best swimmer in the group was Scott's best friend, Jimmy Mathews. Jimmy decided to swim out to the raft to join Scott and the other boys. About twenty yards from the raft, Jimmy developed a cramp and seemed to get caught up in the moss that covered the entire bottom of Home Lake. Scott was horrified when he realized that Jimmy was not going to be able to reach the raft. Although he had no idea of the skill it took to successfully complete a water rescue, Scott jumped into the lake and swam to his friend. By that time, Jimmy was in such a panic and so combative that Scott was unable to rescue him. The memory of that day had remained with Scott for nine years and now that same feeling of helplessness flooded over him as he watched these young soldiers being swept out to sea. Tears ran down his cheeks and he was overwhelmed with grief as Scott turned to Ron, "God help their families," was all that he could think of to say.

Vietnam is a country located in the corner of Southeast Asia. It borders Cambodia on the south and Laos on the north and west. Hanoi is the capital of the country and Ho Chi Minh City, formerly known as Saigon, in the south, is the largest city. Overall, Scott found Vietnam to be a gorgeous country with green hills and lush jungles. At first, the Vietnamese people seemed to welcome the American military to their country. The U.S. had furnished the South Vietnam army with 80% of their equipment. Later, the war turned scary for the American troops because it was impossible to tell who the enemy was. Everyone looked the same! The NVA (North Vietnam Army) and VC (Vietcong) were very well organized, but worse, they were not afraid to die. Scott lost many friends in a failed effort. After this experience, he believed that whenever America becomes involved in a military conflict, Congress should first declare war and give the military the means to end it as soon as possible and not string it out for ten years, with thousands of American lives lost. Like most of those young men who served in Vietnam, Scott knew first-hand the futility of this American incursion into deep and uncharted waters.

From Cam Ranh Bay, Scott and Ron were transported to the Americal Division headquarters at Chu-lai in a troop transport truck. Everything became very real from this point on. Vietnam is a beautiful country. Frequent monsoon rains provided moisture for lush vegetation, but the smell of death continued to detract from the beauty of their surroundings. Scott looked over at Ron and remarked, "This is a little different than our high school football field."

"Ours too," Ron laughed.

They were deployed almost immediately from Chu Lai 35 miles to the north and west to a desolate plateau topped by a lone American outpost. This hill, known to the American troops as landing zone (LZ) Stinson, would become Scott's home base for the next year. The whole time he hoped he wouldn't have to die on that particular piece of real estate. LZ Stinson was a high point in the middle of rain forest. The soldiers lived in straw huts like something you'd see on a deserted island. They were actually Army canvas huts which basically kept out the rain, but since it was always warm, they didn't need any extra heat. When it rained, it was like a shower, so staying dry was a continuous struggle. As an artillery base with several dozen 105 and 155mm cannons, Stinson was a permanent community of 30 to 40 soldiers, and provided a base camp for numbers of Army and Marine infantry. The highlights of the week were letters from home and the delivery of beer sent down from Chu-lai. The landing zone provided a home for the UH-1 (Huey) helicopters used to transport Army and Marine Corps troops in and out of the bush. Unfortunately, they also provided a great target for the North Vietnam Army and VC mortars. At twenty-five, Scott was considered one of the old guys. He was known as "Lamp" because he was assigned to operate a jeep-mounted searchlight. Scott saw many friends killed, but by the grace of God, he survived. He said often, "My heart especially went out to the married guys with children at home." He also saw a lot of guys come to the Lord during those days. Ron and Scott dreaded the search light duty, which was not the safest assignment in Vietnam. The light provided a perfect target for enemy fire.

In mid-August 1970, Scott's heart was broken when Ron was killed by a sapper. A sapper was a Viet Cong who had one mission in mind. They would sneak in under the rolled barbed wire barricade on a suicide mission to kill Americans. Ron was manning the searchlight that night. The sappers carried small bombs similar to grenades. As Ron shone the searchlight, in an effort to aid the fire direction control to locate the VC, a sapper's grenade took his life. Scott grieved as the next day he wrote a long letter to Ron's family explaining how much their friendship had meant while minimizing the details of his death.

Somehow, Scott kept his head low and his wits about him, as the days, then weeks, then months passed by. Combat soldiers see most everything. One particular quality served Scott well during his combat tour. He learned not to take anything personally! Easier said than done, for sure, but his mantra was "what it is, is what it is." Keep on moving, do your job, try to survive, and someday, go home. It's not like he hadn't been shot before.

While sitting alone one night on duty, he remembered back to when he was 19, after downing a late night hamburger and home fries at Monte Vista's favorite greasy spoon; he and four buddies were walking across a street to their cars. As fate would have it, at the same time, a carload of liquor-primed young men from a neighboring town drove by. There was enough bluster in the air to fill most of the Grand Canyon. Comments were made between the two groups about different aspects of their mothers and sisters and then the car turned right and disappeared. Scott and his buddies laughed and decided to go see who was hanging out at the local A & W Root Beer stand. Suddenly, the car re-appeared and quickly approached Scott and his friends. Before he really knew what was happening he heard the "pop, pop, pop" of a .22 caliber hand gun. He saw his buddy Jeff Martin fall to the ground holding his stomach as the car sped off into the dark. Chaos followed with Scott's buddies screaming to get Jeff to the hospital. Gary White, whose nifty, customized '57 Chevy, was parked right in front of the group, was chosen in the heat of battle to drive. His response was, "No way. I don't want all that blood on my new seat covers." Plan B was executed and somehow Jeff made it to the local ER. It was several minutes after Jeff had been taken into the hospital that Scott felt a weird sensation in his left leg. Further inspection revealed a "through and through." He also had been shot. He would live to tell about it and now he was 8,000 miles and half a world removed from the "friendly" confines of home.

One day on LZ Stinson, Scott had a visitor. A lone infantryman came wandering into the camp, asking for him. It was a weird situation for two reasons: one, infantrymen are not usually walking alone through the tall grass of southeast Asia, and two, what were the chances of that same person asking specifically for Scott? Scott made his way to the operations center. His visitor turned out to be none other than Jeff Martin, Scott's drive-by shooting buddy from the streets of Monte Vista. Jeff was "looking for his unit" and somehow found out that Scott was close by. None of this made much sense, but then again, at that point nothing about this war was making much sense – to anyone. Both Scott and Jeff were small-town boys who had seen little of the world and the tour in Southeast Asia was a real eye-opener.

After his war experience, Scott was sure he didn't care much about any place outside the USA, particularly when any fighting was going on. The two Colorado friends laughed and partied for 24 hours. Jeff then sauntered off down the road headed northeast. Both he and Scott made it through their tour in Vietnam without as much as a scratch.

Scott liked his Army job and believed in the American cause, but often wondered if the Viet Cong saw him as a real bright, inviting, and convenient target. "Surely, one of those crazy bastards is trying to put me out of business and win the big prize of the night," he had thought to himself many times. He could vaguely remember the old days at a summer carnival in southern Colorado where he and his high school buddies would target-shoot to win the big teddy bears to give to their current sweethearts. Except this war was neither fun nor a festival, and LZ Stinson was no carnival. In fact, Scott—along with his searchlight—WAS the big prize, the Viet Cong equivalent of the big teddy bear.

Shortly after 2:00 A. M. in the early morning hours of September 7, 1970, on the top of a desolate jungle plateau in the totally alien environment of the central highlands of South Vietnam, 25 year old Army Specialist Reemers was thinking to himself, "What the hell am I doing here? This is not when or where I want to die! And besides that, why do these people always have to attack at 2:00 A.M.?" He didn't have long to think about these or any other meaningless questions. All hell broke loose on his small hill. Gunfire and rocket blasts have a way of focusing one's attention on other issues-like survival and praying. All around him the ground was exploding, the sky was on fire, and men were yelling and screaming at the top of their lungs. LZ Stinson was under attack, again, by hostile forces, called "Charlie" by the Americans. This was his most traumatic night in Vietnam.

Scott's unit was completely surrounded by the VC and the North Vietnam army. They were hitting the Americans with mortars, rockets, and AK Forty-seven automatic weapons. Everyone thought the world was coming to an end. Explosions were happening all around and the noise was like two locomotives hitting head-on mixed with the intermittent popping of the AK Forty-seven's. He knew that his life was now in God's hands, and he was praying constantly while shooting his Quad-Fifty machine gun at any flash in the darkness. After 7 months on the hill Scott had experienced several brief attacks always around 2: 00 A. M., but they seemed to him to be "hit and miss" attempts by roving enemy forces designed more to agitate the Americans than kill them. This night the attack felt different from the start. Decades later Scott would reflect, "It was a particularly quiet night, very still--and pretty spooky. Maybe that is what death feels like." Scott's job was to sit in the back of his CJ-5 Jeep and shine that huge spotlight out into the empty darkness of the jungle. He would peer into the night, scan the surrounding country side, and look for any signs of enemy movement. The Viet Cong would have made the Apache Indians proud with the way they could sneak ever so quietly through the undergrowth. Scott knew that any kind of movement, however subtle, might be a signal of imminent harm to him and his American buddies.

During the frequent enemy raids on his outpost, he would point the big light in the direction of the attackers and hope to illuminate them in the deadly still of the night. That night the rectangular piece of Asian real estate, not much bigger than a football field, was "home" to 123 American Marines and Army troops and about twenty South Vietnamese soldiers. At 1: 59 A. M., Scott was looking at the stars and wondering about past autumns in Colorado. Damned if it wasn't football season again. By 2:02 A. M. he thought the entire North Vietnam army was coming his way; charging hard and ready to kick some American ass! In fact, the entire LZ was under attack by a large number of enemy soldiers. Scott found himself in the middle of that blazing and terrifying experience. While combat mortar rounds, coming from God knows where, were destroying life, limb and property all around him, rifle fire was lighting up the Asian night like hundreds of firecrackers exploding about shoulder height. And it wasn't as if Scott could follow his basic instinct to duck. He was scared, but he couldn't hide under cover or dive into the nearest foxhole. He had to keep his light shining out into the darkness. The Americans were totally surrounded by Charlie. This was not the work of a small band of jungle bandits wanting merely to wake up and piss off the Americans. On this night, these people wanted to do major damage. They just wanted to kill as many Americans as possible.

Wave after wave of enemy troops came charging out of the dark of night with the sole purpose of breaking through the perimeter barriers, over-running the small number of Americans, and reclaiming this particular piece of real estate. This attack, much like the entire Vietnam War, was about claiming-or reclaiming--one hill at a time, if only for a day! Behind the confusion and cover of heavy mortar fire, the Viet Cong soldiers came in mass. Hundreds of guerrilla fighters were streaming out of the dense Asian jungle, running up the 30 degree incline, screaming the screams of crazed combat warriors, firing their rifles, machine guns, and mortars. The craziest of the crazy would come charging full force, yelling cries of vengeance, launching themselves into the thick strands of barbed wire surrounding the LZ. Their purpose was to infiltrate the base, get close enough to use their hand grenades and bayonets, and cut American throats. These suicide "sappers" seldom made it through the heavily guarded perimeter, but when they did, often Americans died. The fight continued, the Viet Cong kept coming, and minutes seemed like hours. Inside the perimeter of LZ Stinson, explosions from artillery and mortar rounds were lighting the sky like a Stephen King Fourth of July, blowing up supply tents, ammo dumps and outhouses. After 20 minutes of constant noise, fire, injury and death, Scott thought this might be the day he would die. He might have seen his last sunrise.

Fortunately for Scott and most of the other 123 Americans manning LZ Stinson, "The Home of Ready Rifles" lived up to its billing on this particular night. M-16s and Quad-50s blazed away. As Charlie would hit the wire and try to twist their way into the interior of the American camp, they would promptly die, courtesy of sharp-shooting U. S. Marines. The entire outlying perimeter was guarded by the Marines, strategically placed to do what Marines do best. They did their job that night and did it well. Time and time again Scott's beam of light would reveal dead or dying Viet Cong, hung up in the thick barbed wire that buffered the LZ from the outside world. He thought to himself, "If I live through this nightmare, I will forever have a fond place in my heart for the US Marines."

On this hot and humid South Vietnam night, when most of America was thinking about war protests, or the upcoming football season, Scott and the rest of the 123 troops on that desolate jungle hill were fighting-and praying for their lives. What Scott was not aware of was the quick-thinking action taken by one of the junior officers within minutes of the initial barrage of explosions. An Army lieutenant had placed a radio call to DaNang calling for assistance from the "Jolly Green Giants."

The Jolly Green Giant

Jolly Green Giants were helicopters with mini-guns mounted on the sides. These mini-guns could put a bullet into every square inch of a football field in ninety seconds. Scott felt tremendous relief as he heard the "whump," "whump," "whump" of the propellers in the distance as they rushed to the battle site. By the grace of God, the Jolly Green Giant would save many American lives that night. After what seemed to be an eternity, but was really about 45 minutes, heaven suddenly opened up for the Americans and all hell descended on Charlie. Suddenly, without warning, the "Jolly Green Giants" appeared out of the dark Asian sky and the two 7.62mm NATO mini-guns opened deadly fire as this Angel of Death swept in and over the enemy forces. Laying down over 2,000 rounds per minute per gun, in addition to pilot-controlled rockets, the life-saving Jolly Green Giants quickly turned the grassy slopes surrounding LZ Stinson into a killing field. As the rumble of the two 1,500 horse-power engines grew louder, Scott knew what was about to happen--at least he was hoping what would happen. He needed to stay alive just a little bit longer. “Please God, just 5 more minutes.”

As quickly as the battle started, it ended. The fighting was over and the night was eerily silent with the exception of men crying out in pain and fear. Charlie was dead, dying, or in hasty retreat. Six Americans were killed that evening and a dozen or so had injuries and wounds that would be their early ticket back to the “real world”. Scott, after all, would live to see another sunrise. Like thousands of U. S. combat troops before and after him, Scott did his job that night, obeyed his orders, and tried to take care of his buddies. Combat troops are not fighting for the flag or country as much as they fight for themselves and their comrades. No words exist that describe combat. Non-combatants have no idea. When the supply tent blew up, Scott saw the medics running to help wounded soldiers and heard their painful cries pierce through the cacophony of the dark chaos. He knew he had lost some friends.

God became real to Scott that night, and he forever forged a place in his heart and soul for American military combat veterans. As the sun came up, the Americans who made it through the night shook hands and held each other. They would be forever changed, some for the good, some not so good. The horrors of combat are known only to those who have lived through it. Many times the body, mind, and spirit of the war veteran remain intact and life continues on afterward in a seemingly uninterrupted way. Or at least that's what it looks like from the outside. For many others, the horrors of that experience take their toll--in many different forms. As Scott looked around and saw the wounded and traumatized being airlifted by medivac helicopters off LZ Stinson, little did he know that he would later spend over three decades of his life helping military veterans overcome the physical and emotional consequences of one of man's ugliest behaviors. He did not realize he would be helping hundreds, perhaps thousands, of veterans re-learn how to socialize and readjust to home life. Later he would become a recreational therapist in the Veterans Administration hospital system and serve proudly in that capacity for 30 years. "Recreation." "Re-Create." Learn to laugh, work and play again. Fill the head and heart with something other than pain and nightmares.

Scott survived the night attack on LZ Stinson in one piece. He would stay there for the remainder of his tour in Vietnam. Originally, his tour of duty "in country" was to be 12 months. Under normal discharge conditions, following his return to the U.S. he would be obligated for two years of the Army Reserves following active duty. However, while still in Vietnam and in a moment of whiskey-induced bravado and a "short-timers" attitude, Scott and two of his buddies reenlisted for an extra two months to be served in Vietnam-in exchange for no reserve duty if and when they got back to the States. The next morning following this ill-conceived "re-up"-and especially on the morning of his originally scheduled departure date, December 24, Scott once again was wondering, "What in hell was I thinking?" It had dawned on him that statistically most of the combat causalities in Vietnam occurred either in the first two or the last two months of duty. Rookie mistakes or short-timer mistakes! Anyway, it was too late now. He would spend 60 of the longest days of his life completing his assignment in Southeast Asia. Scott hoped he wouldn't become another statistic. But at least this way if he did make it home he would be discharged immediately rather than being stationed at yet another military base back in the States. Everyday Scott had a little more doubt about the decision to extend especially when two friends, Jessie and Mike were killed during the same extension period.

February 24 finally arrived and Scott flew home to Colorado. He could never find the words to express his joy the moment the troop transport plane lifted off the ground in Cam Ranh Bay. That day was filled with sheer joy and relief as well as the mixed feelings of sadness and concern for the buddies that would not be making that flight home. The Huey came to pick Scott up from LZ Stinson that day to fly into Chu-Lai and on to Cam Ranh Bay. From there he flew on a commercial airliner to Fort Lewis, Washington. The atmosphere on the trip home was 180 degrees different from the trip over. There was much laughter and a multitude of war stories. There was singing and joking, but also tears of joy and sorrow for those that had been left behind and those that would never return. When Scott arrived at Fort Lewis, the first thing he did was to kneel down and kiss the ground. The second thing was to find a flush toilet. Scott's great lesson from Vietnam was that the real heroes of this country are not on the playing fields, in movie theaters, or on T.V. screens. They are the men and women who serve in distant lands, often under terrible conditions and who sometimes are called on to make the supreme sacrifice. When he arrived home, Scott had little idea that his connection with military veterans was just beginning.

Chapter 2

When Scott Reemers and most other Vietnam vets re-entered civilian life in the 1970's, there were no "heroes' welcomes," no parades of honor, no recognition of a "job well done." In fact, his discharge somewhat coincided with the shooting of five students by National Guard troops on the campus of Kent State University during a student protest against U.S. involvement in Vietnam. In the turmoil of war protests, combat vets often bore the brunt of angry discontent and hostile rhetoric from any civilian who thought their opinion mattered. At home, Scott unpacked his duffel bag, put on his t-shirt and jeans, and once again became a college student. He re-enrolled in Adams State College and went about the business of securing a master's degree in physical education and recreation. As a former high school athlete, he figured maybe he could someday coach and teach physical education.

Since he was getting veterans' benefits while going to school, he enrolled in a recreation studies master's degree program. One day, more than likely on the way to the student center to shoot some pool, he filled out a federal government employment application, not giving it an ounce of thought after he put the pen down. Most of Scott's classmates were unemployed coaches from high schools or junior colleges who needed an advanced degree just to qualify for a coaching position. He talked to them each day at class, worried about his chances, with no real experience, at getting even an assistant coach's job. He also worried about what his mentor at school had told him about planning to move at least eight times during his coaching career.

Then the darnest thing happened. The U. S. government wrote and offered him a job! Or maybe not a job, but at least an interview for a job in a Veterans' Administration (VA) Hospital located somewhere in Wyoming. For both Scott and his new wife, Kate, "surprise" was followed first by "disbelief" and eventually by "curiosity." Neither Scott nor Kate knew anything about the VA or Wyoming. Scott had held a number of jobs since he was 15. One of his favorites was working for his grandfather as a delivery man for a local furniture store. However, he knew that lifting heavy furniture for minimum wages was not for him. After his Army experience, he looked forward to a new adventure. In the spring of 1972, Scott and Kate left Alamosa and headed north to begin the 655 mile journey to a new beginning that would open the doors to a new life that would fill the next 30+ years. He told Kate this would be a new beginning in the wilds of "cowboy" country. Kate wasn't so sure. In reality, Scott was thankful just to have a chance at any job that even came close to his recreation therapist specialty.

In just over two hundred years, the United States developed from a sparsely populated, newly discovered territory along the Atlantic into the most powerful country in the world. This journey of expansion, growth, development, and maturity continues to this day to involve many challenges and--at times--violence, both external and internal in nature. Human beings have found reasons to fight and kill each other since the beginning of time and continue to do so. More than likely, cave men fought each other over the rights to the stream, the wild game, or the next cave. Wars and other conflicts have accompanied every single generation. However, history books paint an often abstract and sometimes detached view of those battles but that is not always the real story. It is easy enough to say that nearly 60,000 American service men and women were killed in Vietnam or that over 4,000 American soldiers have been killed in Iraq since 2003. But ask any man or woman who has actually been in combat about the experience. Or ask any spouse or family member who has "welcomed home" their loved one--dead or alive-- from battle, what it meant to them and the story will be anything but impersonal. The real story of war is the price individual fighting men and women--and their families--pay to accomplish valiant and dangerous military duties to protect those of us at home. Often, soldiers pay with their lives. And, for those who do return home, no one is the same person he or she was before they left.

Since the American Revolution over 42 million men and women have served in the Armed Forces during wartime. During that same time, over 650,000 battle deaths have been recorded. Another 525,000 deaths have occurred to military personnel both in theater and non-theater. Nearly 1½ million soldiers received non-mortal wounds. Today there are over 16 ½ million living war veterans. Another eight million living veterans have served in times of peace. Governments in America have offered support to military veterans since 1636. The roots of the current veteran assistance programs first began when the Pilgrims of Plymouth Colony, at war with the Pequot

Indians, passed a law providing that disabled soldiers would be supported by the Colony. The Continental Congress of 1776 encouraged enlistments during the Revolutionary War by promising pensions for soldiers who were disabled. Early in this country's history, medical and hospital care for veterans was provided by state and local communities. The first federally funded medical facility for U. S. military veterans was authorized in 1811. Later in the 19th century veteran benefits were expanded to include widows and dependents. Between the Civil War and World War I state veteran "homes" provided most of the medical and hospital assistance for veterans and their families.

When the United States entered World War I in 1917, Congress established a new system of veterans' benefits. Programs were included for disability compensation, insurance for service persons and veterans, and vocational rehabilitation for the disabled. In the 1920's three separate federal agencies administrated the various benefits: the Veterans Bureau, the Bureau of Pensions of the Interior Department, and the National Home for Disabled Volunteer Soldiers. In 1930, Congress authorized President Herbert Hoover to "consolidate and coordinate government activities affecting war veterans." The new Veterans Administration absorbed the three bureaus. Brigadier General Frank T. Hines, the first Administrator of Veteran Affairs, held the job until 1945. By 1930 the VA health care system had 54 hospitals. World War II resulted in not only a vast increase in the veteran population but also a large number of new benefits for veterans enacted by Congress. On June 22, 1944, the GI Bill, which began paying veterans' unemployment and educational expenses, was signed into law. The GI Bill is thought to have had more influence on the American way of life than any other law since the Homestead Act of 1862 gave land in the American west to millions of pioneers. In 1973, the Veterans Administration assumed the responsibility from the Department of the Army for the National Cemetery System. With the exception of Arlington National Cemetery, all state and national cemetery operations are now managed by the Veterans Administration.

The Department of Veterans Affairs (VA) was established as a Cabinet-level position on March 15, 1989. President George H. Bush said at the time, “There is only one place for the veteran’s affairs of America, and that is in the Cabinet Room, at the table with the President of the United States.” The promise of the expanded Veterans Administration into a Cabinet-level agency has been bitter-sweet for America. On the positive side the VA continues to reflect an ongoing concern and care for America's military veterans. The downside is that there is still a need for such services. Large numbers of veterans suggests large numbers of wars and military conflicts. As of 2005 there were 1,140 various VA sites in the United States. Included in this number, were administrative offices, hospitals, outpatient clinics, and cemeteries. Every state in the Union has VA facilities of some type. One such facility at Fort Mackenzie in Sheridan, Wyoming, had brought Scott Reemers back into the lives of veterans and, in fact, they became his life’s work in a very real and meaningful way.

Sheridan, Wyoming sits in the eastern shadow of the majestic Big Horn Mountains, a 60 million year old range of snow-capped peaks covering over one million acres of exquisite, raw beauty. With a population of over 15,000, Sheridan, originally a frontier outpost named for Civil War hero, General Phil Sheridan, offered supplies to young men and women going west. It has remained economically viable over the years with an economy fueled by the abundant availability of significant sources of energy. Massive coal beds and vast reservoirs of natural gas lie just beneath the surface of the entire region. Despite the chaos that very often accompanies energy "booms," Sheridan has maintained a quaint and quiet sense of community, anchored for over a century by the existence of "The Fort."

Downtown Sheridan Wyoming

"The Fort," now known as the Sheridan Veterans Medical Center, a 296-acre campus containing 65 buildings, sits on a hill overlooking the town. Long before the facility became the site of healing and help for American veterans, it served as the last armed garrison and command post in the Northwest. It was the command center in the United States government's campaign to keep peace between west-bound settlers and the Crow, Cheyenne, and Sioux Indian tribes who had called the area "home" for millennia. At the end of the 19th century, the Army suggested the need for a new post to manage and protect the region's vast forest resources. In the true entrepreneurial spirit of the American system, local Sheridan businessmen lobbied Congress intensely and appropriations were granted for the post in 1898. Soldiers had money. Money meant business.

Fort Mackenzie

Fort Mackenzie was named after a decorated Army general named Ronald S. Mackenzie who earned his reputation by leading soldiers in the Civil War and later in settling what some historians called "Indian troubles" in the Southwest. Mackenzie died in 1888 at the age of 48 of syphilis, going insane in the latter stages of the disease. Fort Mackenzie would eventually become a military hospital, a place of treatment for hundreds of men and women who also had served their country and required help in dealing with the aftermath of combat stress, battle trauma, social reorientation, and numerous manifestations of mental illness.

The effects of war do not stop once a soldier leaves the battlefield. Many battles have been relived over the years within the walls of the Sheridan VA Medical Center. In those days, the medical center was a world apart from the town of Sheridan. The local townspeople had no idea exactly what went on with the patients at the facility. Most thought the hospital was more like a prison for mentally ill veterans. In fact, as late as the early 1970's, most modern treatments for mental illnesses and the wide variety of helpful medications available today were not regularly used as part of the treatment regimen at the hospital.

Scott and Kate Reemers left Alamosa, Colorado, in June, 1972, headed to Wyoming on their way to begin his career as a recreational therapist at the Veterans Hospital.

Scott and Kate's Journey to Wyoming

The Reemers left the familiar sights of Colorado Springs and Denver. After another 100 miles they crossed the

Colorado-Wyoming border, stopped to put gas in the car, and were nearly blown away by the fierce prairie winds. They were in Cheyenne and as sure as the sun coming up in the east, the wind blows in Cheyenne. Kate remarked that she really wasn't sure this trip was such a good idea. The Reemers got back in their car, and pressed onward, looked for signs of life and hoping that the new job would make this all worthwhile. They headed north toward Sheridan. They almost turned around in a desolate place called Chugwater, a little town in the middle of nowhere.

At this point Kate said, "There is no way I'm going to live in this barren place." The land seemed bleak and lifeless to them after coming from southern Colorado. The San Luis Valley, "home" to both Scott and Kate, is surrounded by beautiful mountain ranges on three sides. In fact, Kate's parents would often take their entire family of six westward from Monte Vista, driving a quick 30 minutes into the beautiful scenery and pristine streams of the San Juan Mountains. So far in Wyoming they had seen no trees, no mountains and nothing green for hundreds of miles.

Neither Scott nor Kate had ever been to Wyoming. As they saw the sign welcoming them to their new home state, Kate could only hope that their final destination, Sheridan, would somehow be different. Except for attending Cheyenne's Frontier Days Celebration each

July or friends taking classes at the University of Wyoming, they knew few people who had even been to Wyoming. Surely, beauty is in the eye of the beholder, but the prairie sagebrush and flying dust of central and eastern Wyoming, somewhere north of Laramie, requires a native's eye—or a jackrabbit's sense of home—to appreciate!

If for no other reason than they had absolutely nowhere else to go at the time, the Reemers did not turn around but kept the car heading north. After what seemed like days, Scott and Kate passed the eastbound turnoff to Gillette, Wyoming, natural gas capital of the United States, and saw the first glimmer of hope and the faint outline of—yes, a mountain range. As they arrived in Buffalo, Wyoming, 45 miles south of Sheridan, they could clearly see the beautiful Big Horn Mountains in the distance. It was love at first sight, perhaps magnified by the less-than-green "scenery" that had dominated most of their trip up to that point.

Big Horn Mountains

What a refreshing sight for the travelers after the dull landscape they had been experiencing for days. They arrived finally in Sheridan and fell in love with the area right away. Scott started concentrating on his job interview, scheduled for 9:00 A.M. the next morning.

Scott was so nervous about his first real job interview that he spent the majority of the time on the long sojourn from Alamosa to Sheridan actually looking at notes from his recreation classes. He had committed to memory various teaching strategies, organizational plans, and treatments recommended by the academics of his chosen field. He wanted to make a good impression on his interviewer, Harry Shell. In 1972, Harry was Chief of Recreational Services at the Sheridan facility and surprised Scott right from the beginning by inviting Kate to attend the interview. Even more perplexing to Scott was the fact that Harry seemed more interested in talking to Kate and, at least to Scott, "seemed more interested in discussing the great weather in Sheridan than the requirements of the hospital's recreation program." To this day, Scott gives Kate a large part of the credit for getting the job. From that day forward, she supported him in his career, sometimes just by listening to his tales of unruly patients and disgruntled staff members.

During the interview he almost talked himself out of the job! They went to the V.A. canteen, where he tried to tell Shell about his qualifications. "Here I was, trying to impress Harry with all I knew about recreation therapy, and he was taking us around the hospital, showing us the sights, buying us lunch, and talking about the hot summer temperatures," recalled Scott, who on that day knew absolutely nothing about the Veterans Administration system. Harry was more interested in just filling the civil service position than in Scott's ideas about recreation therapy. It was some time before Scott came to fully appreciate what Harry was doing that day. He was not hiring a "recreational therapist" whose ideas and thoughts and theories would help the veterans. He was hiring a young man who had a dream to create a life with a partner who appeared to want the same thing. He was hiring the heart and soul of a caring person who could, and would, spend countless hours, not just implementing academic theories, but simply talking with and caring about the thousands of patients with whom he would come into contact. Scott was offered the job that day, accepted the position, and was back on the road to Colorado the next day to prepare for a permanent move. Somehow, the landscape looked much better on the return to Colorado. Fort MacKenzie had brought Scott Reemers back into the lives of veterans and they would soon become a major part of his life.

In the 1970's, they were known as recreation specialists instead of the "therapists" of today. Some of the staff actually had degrees in recreation which meant they were more comfortable refereeing volleyball games than actually doing any kind of patient therapy. But despite their knowledge shortcomings, most were dedicated people with a vision of being true "professionals" and making a difference with the veterans under their care. Scott remembered his first assignment, along with two other specialists, to take some ice cream treats over to the geriatric unit. This did not seem too difficult and at least it was some kind of responsibility. What a sight to see three recreation professionals carrying ice cream over to the patient wards and thinking they were really doing something special! These days were later known as the apples and oranges days because every other day they were assigned to take bags of fruit to the patients. They found out that it was extremely important to get the same amount of fruit to each ward or the fight was on!

In time these young staff members became really frustrated! They were craving any form of meaningful activity. Scott was so desperate for responsibility that he volunteered to coach the patient softball team. He had learned coaching methods in school and was anxious to put his skills to good use. There were eight town teams in Sheridan, so the veterans played against the teams in the city. Most of his players had not played softball in 20 years, not to mention the average age was 40 years old! They lost their first 28 games. Their goal was not to have the 10-run rule called on them, ending the game in disgrace. When you are coaching first base and there are two outs you tell your runner "There are two outs so run on anything." Scott told his first runner this and the man just took off running even before the pitch! He knew it was going to be a long season!

Scott liked his first supervisor, but Harry didn't know much about recreation therapy. Harry was a grandfatherly type who had no real feel for modern therapy methods. Despite his great personality, Harry was "old school" as far as patient treatment. In the summer he wanted Scott to play human chessmen with the patients outdoors in 100 degree heat. Scott soon discovered this did not work with Thorazine patients. Thorazine is used for the treatment of schizophrenia (severe disruptions in thought and perception). It is also prescribed for the short-term treatment of severe behavioral disorders. The drug's numerous, sometimes disruptive side effects are not readily compatible with a mild game of chess. Scott was thankful when he finally got his first assignment to a specific unit. This meant he was out from under Harry's direct control and could apply a little of what he had learned in school. He was assigned to the drug and alcohol ward. It was a real understatement to say that both staff and patients were "laid back". After a few meetings he figured out that the only difference between the staff and the patients was that the patients sometimes got better! For the first 15 years with the VA he worked with drug and alcohol patients. These veterans came from all professions and ranged in age from 19 to 80 years. Some had come from living on the streets of Denver to being a part of a patient softball team. Just to be part of a group that wore the same team shirts was a major step forward.

Sheridan VA Medical Facility

In the 1950's and 60's, the Sheridan VA Medical Center's main patient facilities consisted of locked psychiatric units. There were guards posted at the entrance gate. All wards were locked and few medications were administered. There were no recreation services or recreation specialists. Any recreation activities that occurred were conducted by the nursing assistants in the special services division. All such activities took place on the hospital grounds. No off-station activities were allowed, nor at that time were any activities conducted by outside volunteers.

On the few occasions when there was an activity such as a movie, all patients attended. Nursing assistants were expected to march a unit down to the auditorium acting as guards. Patients from each ward were forced to sit in their own section and were marched back to their wards at the end of the activity. The nursing assistants, who were like prison guards, were expected to use any means necessary to capture or restrain out-of-control patients and return them to their ward. These assistants, mostly men, would have been right at home as bouncers in the local bars. Also common were electric shock treatments and frontal lobotomies, methods often used to control the behavior of patients. Many employees lived on a residential ward during their work week and returned to their homes and families on the weekends. There was a story told of a patient going into the employees' residential ward with a pipe and beating a nursing assistant to death because of the way the nursing assistant had restrained him earlier.

When Scott came to the V. A. Hospital in 1972, the nursing assistants were no longer expected to conduct recreational activities for the patients. Administrators had come to recognize the fact that leisure time activities were an integral part of an effective therapeutic program and that professionals were needed to make the program work. By this time there was an established Volunteer

Services/Recreation department. Patients were treated more humanely and had much more freedom to come and go as they pleased and medications were being used much more effectively to assist in managing behavior. Later, the employees in the recreation department were all college graduates who were considered professional recreational therapists. As therapists, their job was to be a part of the unit treatment team and to assist in preparing patients for functioning outside of the VA hospital. Initially, however, they often found themselves planning and running social events rather than carrying out treatment plans for individual patients.

The frustration of this dilemma was alleviated when the Director of Recreation at the central office in Washington, D. C. required therapists to become members of the NTRS (National Therapeutic Recreation Society) which certified recreation therapists as professional medical personnel. After that, they were then more readily accepted as a true part of the therapeutic team. They became part of the Rehab Medicine Service which put them in the same category as speech therapists, physical therapists, occupational therapists, and educational therapists. This nation-wide effort brought acknowledgment of recreational therapists as professional staff and as an integral part of the medical treatment team. They had come from a point of chasing out-of-control patients across a field and tackling them to becoming part of an interdisciplinary treatment community.

Hank Farrow joined the recreation staff in the early 1980's. Hank was 6' 4" and had played big time college football. He had a real love of his job and was always kind to his patients. He always had a good word and a pat on the back for anyone who needed just a little extra encouragement. As the first staff member to have a degree in recreational therapy, he brought in programs such as re-socialization groups, leisure education, and challenge courses. He also brought recognition of individual needs and compassion for veteran patients. This marked a great advancement for the recreational department toward the development of a truly professional program. By this time, the therapists were able to employ work study students from the local college to handle the diversional activities, allowing the therapists to conduct truly therapeutic treatments with patients.

Lucy Martin joined the staff soon after Hank. Lucy was a truly gorgeous woman, so she was always a favorite with the male patients. But, Lucy was all business on the job. She had a therapeutic recreation degree from Central Michigan University, and was able to introduce many therapeutic programs to the geriatric unit. Her love and dedication to these older veterans was an inspiration to the entire department. She had a real affinity for the older patients. She seemed to pick out the most fragile and neglected individuals, those that no one else really wanted to treat. She would give a big hug to even the most unappealing patient just to raise their spirits. Needless to say, there was heavy competition for one of Lucy's hugs. Through the years, Scott, Hank and Lucy became great friends, each bringing their own strengths to the department. They took great pride in the quality of the program that they were able to provide to the veteran patients.

Throughout the 1970's, Scott grew as a professional and gained confidence in his ability to be an effective, participating member of the total treatment program. In the 1980's this professional expertise enabled the creation of formal classes and other learning opportunities to prepare veterans to function in the community rather than within an institutional setting. In the 1990's the department changed from a full therapeutic recreation program to a partial program due to the reformation of the VA system and the decline in the number of resident patients.

As Scott looked back, he had a feeling of fulfillment, pride and reward for the opportunity to help provide recreational services for the deserving men and women from our armed services. At the VA Medical Center he worked with Dan Pride, who was the chief of Recreation Therapy. He also worked with Lucy and Hank as the key members of the recreation therapy staff. These were four people with the same goal – to help the veterans obtain good mental health, physical health and social skills. Over time each recognized there were many different approaches to achieving this goal and that each patient had his own special story.

Chapter 3

After many years of working with veterans, Scott came to realize the importance of treating his recreation therapy patients, not just as sick or disabled, but as individuals with problems driven by their experiences in combat or in many cases, their inability to adjust to the "normality" of day-to-day life upon returning home. His own experience in Vietnam had given him an insight into the many difficulties faced by returning vets. He determined early in his career to use his own experiences with the problems of readjusting to family and civilian life in general to try to relate to others. Scott found his years of working with alcohol and drug, psychiatric, geriatric, dementia, and Alzheimer's patients very rewarding. You had to love some of the things they would say or do. Many veterans were very intelligent and well spoken. They all had different stories and interesting histories. Scott and his fellow staff members knew that every veteran who came to the VA for help was there for a reason. Their problems were not always evident on the surface. Sometimes the pressures and circumstances that drove a veteran to seek help were not readily apparent. Often the veteran simply had no place else to go.

The recreation therapy staff at the Sheridan Medical Center always tried to treat the veteran patient as an individual and not merely a number to be typed, cataloged and put into a computer. In multi-disciplinary team meetings, they would start with the medical diagnosis but they always wanted to go deeper into the patient's history, personality and his own special needs. The staff would conduct a pre-interview with the veteran before forming a treatment plan. Each veteran had his/her own individual story. Scott and the others realized it was particularly important to really understand what the veteran had experienced during and after his or her military time.

When Scott arrived at the Medical Center in 1972 there was one of thirteen Spanish American War veterans. Bill was 105 years old. Also there was John Wells, one of the few surviving World War I veterans. John was 85 years old when Scott first met him. He was in the geriatric unit and lived there 365 days a year. John had outlived all of his family and friends. He yearned, day in and day out, for something to do. At that time recreation activities were focused totally on diversional types of programs. There was really no prescribed "medical" treatment programming and certainly no real consultation between physicians and the recreational therapists. For patients like John there were no formal recreational treatment plans. Scott remembered these as the bowling and bingo days. Of course, there was no concept of off-station recreation activities. John came from a generation that really appreciated anything the VA could do for them. In 1972, they were still called VA "Hospitals" and not yet designated as "Medical Centers," and for patients like John, the "hospital" was more like a prison. Of course he could leave, but after spending 52 years of his life there, leaving didn't seem to make much sense.

John loved bowling. It was his only real activity aside from eating and sleeping. What made this interesting was that he had only two toes! No one was quite sure how this had happened. Maybe it had been a war injury? No one really cared, but it assured John's status as a disabled veteran. Although his toeless condition must have made bowling uncomfortable to say the least, he very seldom missed a bowling session. The VA bowling alley had manual pin setters. There were no such things as automatic pin setting machines. John would curse softly to himself if the pin setter failed to set up the next frame quickly. To Scott, John was a great example of the good work the VA Center could accomplish. He believed that veterans like John somehow deserved a fair share of care and dignity in their final years. John passed away in 1978 and is buried on the Medical Center grounds. Scott and a few of the staff were the only ones at his last service. It was to be the first of many such events Scott would attend over the years. For him, each one was special.

As time passed, older veterans became fewer in number at the VA Center. Still, Scott noticed a re-occurring pattern in their problems. Those with physical disabilities became fewer in number while medical conditions associated with the long term psychological effects of war emerged in greater numbers. Among World War II veterans, alcohol and drug abuse cases increased significantly as these veterans grew older. Perhaps their problems had been hidden for years just below the surface.

Frank Rosenberg was a World War II veteran who, at age 70, found himself in the Center's Alcohol and Drug Unit. Frank had begun to be a problem drinker after his retirement from an insurance company in Denver. His family used his VA benefits as a way to escape the daily trauma and costs of living with an alcoholic. After many long discussions with Frank, Scott found that his problems could be traced back to his experiences at the end of the war. They had many discussions about the horrors that he had seen as part of the liberation of the concentration camp at Dachau in Germany. The vision of the gaunt faces of the few survivors and the emaciated bodies of the victims had haunted him unrelentingly for thirty years. Frank loved baseball and was the left fielder on the V.A. softball team. During practice sessions, Scott and Frank had often talked of his feelings of guilt for the millions of Jewish victims of that German nightmare. Scott tried to reassure Frank that he certainly had no reason for guilt, but to Frank his remembrance of the death camp was as real as if it had happened only a few days before. Scott soon realized that Frank's battle with alcoholism was only a symptom of deep seated feelings of guilt and inadequacy in dealing with the horror or the Holocaust he had seen firsthand. After several discussions with the assigned physician, Scott was able to arrange Frank's transfer to the psychiatric unit. Six months later, Scott was happy to learn that Frank had been discharged and was returning home to his family. Scott continued to receive a Hanukkah card from Frank for many years.

In the early 1980's, the recreation therapists were allowed to introduce off-site excursions as part of the patient treatment protocol. In addition to providing more diversions from the daily routine, the off-site trips always provided an excellent opportunity for more personal interaction with the patients. During several of these activities, Scott remembered his discussions with Bob Moore, who suffered with a severe anxiety disorder stemming from the onset of Alzheimer's. Bob had fought at Normandy on the north coast of France. He was there on D-day, June 6, 1944, when the Allied forces took 9,500 casualties. Knowing that Scott had also experienced combat and lost friends seemed to make it easier for him to open up and discuss his feelings about that day.

Bob was 65 years old when he came to the Alzheimer's unit. Alzheimer's is thought to be due to two main forms of neural damage. Nerve fibers grow tangled, and protein deposits, known as plaques, build up in the affected tissue. Alzheimer's disease is incurable; however, certain medications seem to slow its progress. The disease is very sad for the family. Bob, in the later stages, did not know his wife of 35 years. In his first several years at the Center, Bob could still drive a car, but he would forget how to get back to the VA. The good part was that he would usually drive to the same place. So, when the police were called, they would know where to go to get him. Bob was a World War II veteran with several combat medals. He was always friendly with other patients and staff, but would get frustrated with his inability to remember names and places and even how to do simple daily activities.

Bob's favorite activity was going on the off-station van rides. The Alzheimer's patients always enjoyed these rides. They would usually start at the elk pasture. Each week they would ask where the elk had come from! The therapist would repeat the same story each time but no one seemed to mind. This group of patients was just happy to get out of the unit and into the open air. They appreciated everything that was done for them even though they might not remember. In addition to the trips off-station, the recreational therapists often took Alzheimer's patients on walks. Studies have shown that exercise may stimulate the area of the brain that is linked to speech. It is important to talk to these patients because it is believed that it will help preserve long term memory. Scott enjoyed working with this type of patient as every small pleasure seemed like real progress. As Bob's condition worsened over several years, Scott knew that the final result was inevitable. In the end, Bob did not recognize his family or even the staff who attended him daily. On the day he passed away, he talked briefly to Scott about his experiences at Normandy. His last thoughts were of his friends lost so many years before. He slipped away quietly that evening.

Over his thirty years at the Medical Center, about 80% of Scott's patients were from the Vietnam era. Nearly all had mental rather than physical problems. Many of these vets had been under attack in the infamous Tet Offensive of 1968. In March of that year, nearly every American location was hit by the North Vietnamese Army or the Viet Cong. Many patients had spent years self-medicating in order to forget those horrible experiences. As a result, drug and alcohol abuse was highest in this group. These patients were by far the most active in the recreation program. Their ages ranged from nineteen years to sixty years, and they were eager to participate in nearly any activity just to keep their minds focused on the present. Remembering his time in Vietnam, Scott could always identify with the problems faced by those who went through the trauma of that long war.

After World War II, veterans having persistent and disturbing mental pictures of events occurring during combat were thought to have a condition known as "shell shock." During and after the Vietnam era, veterans with these same symptoms had "flashbacks." Flashbacks may consist of images, sounds, smells, or feelings, and are often triggered by ordinary occurrences, such as a door slamming or a car backfiring on the street. A person having a flashback may lose touch with reality and believe that the traumatic incident is happening all over again. Regardless of the name, the effects of this traumatic psychological phenomenon continue to impact many hundreds of veterans to this day.

Mental health workers observing veterans returning from recent conflicts in the Middle East are also reporting similar cases among those veterans. At the Sheridan VA Medical Center, Scott, Lucy, and Hank became key members of a medical treatment team along with a psychiatrist, psychologist, medical doctors, social workers, and other medical personnel. Veterans with these "flashbacks" or similar long-term effects of combat exposure were assigned to the treatment team for intensive therapy. This diagnosis is difficult to treat because of the severity and frequency of these mental conflicts. The cases ranged from mild irritation to overt violence or suicidal tendencies. In response, the recreation therapy staff developed various kinds of leisure education classes and other activities to help divert the patients' feelings to less disruptive areas of attention. Often these activities were designed to provide opportunities within the Medical Center community that could more productively occupy the veteran's thoughts and divert their minds from their memories of war.

Of the many challenges facing the recreation staff, none was more difficult than attempting to help veterans trying to conquer or sometimes, just to live with, their combat induced psychological disorders. Each case was different and no single solution could address every set of symptoms. The first few years after the fall of South Vietnam and the American evacuation of the country in 1974 saw many returning veterans, some unable to cope with re-entry into civilian life. Scott had told Hank and Lucy how thankful he was to have come back from Vietnam to a loving family and a great opportunity to make a full and useful life. He was sure his finding spiritual peace in those far-off jungles really meant the difference between him and some of those less fortunate veterans.

Often, the veteran's inner conflicts surfaced in the form of anger and aggression. In late 1974, Scott worked with a young man from Salt Lake City named Tom Waters. Scott suggested that Tom sign on to the veterans' softball team. At first, Tom was full of rage. He hated his experiences in the war and could not understand why America had let this terrible injustice occur. Everyone was to blame. This rage was directed toward staff, coaches, teammates and the world in general. Knowing of Tom's knowledge of softball, Scott took a chance and put Tom in the position of player/coach. Tom showed his appreciation for Scott's willingness to take this chance by making a concerted effort to control his rage as he took his responsibilities as assistant coach very seriously. Slowly, with the help of the staff and to some extent, his fellow patients, Tom was able to better control his emotions. In time his anger subsided. Today he lives a productive life with his family in Utah. Tom came to the realization that some things simply cannot be changed and he must learn to live in an imperfect world.

By 1978, the techniques used by the therapists were becoming more sophisticated. Scott worked with another "flashback" patient named Mike. The medical team determined that Mike was an ideal candidate for their new Intensive Therapy Program, known as the ITP. Mike was a natural leader but had lost his confidence as a result of his persistent disturbing visions of his combat experiences. To Mike his visions seemed real. Often he would have particularly bad days and would become immersed in one traumatic episode after another. On better days he seemed to behave normally, but his symptoms were never far from the surface. The ITP was designed as an intensive diversion program. The patient would be assigned to several recreation activities in sequence under the supervision of the recreation therapist. While the regimen could seem brutal, its purpose was to refocus the patient's mental faculties on tough physical activity in order to minimize the "down" time available for too much thinking. Mike complained bitterly to Scott that he was being singled out for too much work. This made Scott and the other therapists put on the pressure even more. They knew that Mike's resentment at being "picked on" could help substitute for the more intense emotions of his "flashbacks." As part of the ITP, Mike would be given the responsibility for supervising physical exercise activities involving other veterans. As the therapists had hoped, Mike soon felt more confident in supervising the exercises of other patients and was better able to release his anxieties through his own physical activity. After several months of the intermittent ITP program in combination with the new anti-depressant medications that were coming into use, Mike managed to better control his emotions and the visions gradually disappeared. He left the Medical Center in 1979 and became a successful businessman in Phoenix, Arizona.

Phil Morris came to the VA from Cheyenne, Wyoming in 1975. He was an ex-marine who had real anger issues from his time in Southeast Asia. He was 30 years old and built solidly through years of hard exercise. He also had an ex-wife who said his anger was the main reason for their divorce. He was very abusive to people around him, and had a very difficult time complying with his treatment team plan. He had many verbal and even physical conflicts with the staff.

Surprisingly, Phil was an educated man with a degree in recreation. The staff designed Phil's treatment plan to attempt to use his education to help the recreation program. At first they made him the assistant coach of the VA patient softball team. This did not work as he quickly got into conflicts with the other patients on the team. The staff had high hopes for Phil as he seemed to have a lot of potential. However, he could not seem to overcome his anger control issues. Hank Farrow was excellent with working with this type of patient. He put Phil on the paid ITP program, and Phil seemed to show signs of progress. He liked the recreation staff, but continued to have problems with the medical staff members on the psychiatric unit.

Sadly, at that time, the condition known as Post Traumatic Stress Disorder was virtually unknown among the VA medical community. The PTSD program had not yet been adopted at the VA Medical Center. Phil Morris was one of those unfortunate veterans for whom the VA's adoption of more modern mental health treatment came too late. Phil was ultimately discharged from the Center in 1977 with little progress in treating his misunderstood condition. Several years later a staff follow–up on Phil showed that he was not able to adjust to living in society and was ultimately arrested for domestic violence and ended up in prison. It was truly unsettling and sad for the recreation staff to see someone with his knowledge and talent so controlled by his anger.

Hank was one of the best recreation therapists ever to work at the Sheridan Center. He was physically a giant of a man but inside was very gentle. His imposing physique made him a commanding presence among the patients. After extended periods in the wards, the veterans could be counted on to test the patience and determination of the staff whenever possible. Scott and the other main therapist, Lucy, learned quickly that almost any situation could be resolved quickly when Hank was on your side. Despite his physical size, Hank had a way of getting inside the heads of some of the most disturbed patients. His knowledge of the outdoors, wildlife, sports and nature made him ideally suited for relating to veterans and their problems. Veterans were encouraged to express their feelings about their problems without fear of judgment or embarrassment. They learned about expressing themselves in a group of peers and often developed the ability to express their thoughts ranging from general anxiety to opening up about more personal feelings. Frequently, guilt was the feeling being repressed. Many veterans felt guilty about their comrades who had not survived the war. Hank understood that the freedom to express these feelings was very therapeutic to the veterans. He was particularly attentive to the Center's disabled veterans and would always work to ensure their special needs come first.

In 1982, Hank began working with Jim Cramer, whose continuing memories of combat experiences had led to years of severe depression. When Jim arrived at the Center he had already been treated with nearly every drug known to the medical profession. Undoubtedly, this continued medical cocktail had done more harm than good. The doctors had essentially given up; but Hank thought he would try a different approach. He worked with Jim daily for weeks to rid his mind and body of the effects of years of drug over-use. As Jim slowly responded, Hank developed a nature awareness program he thought might help alleviate Jim's bouts of depression.

At first, Jim wanted no part of Hank's ideas. Hank worked with him for nearly four months and eventually was able to convince Jim to participate in what the therapists called the outrigger program. This treatment involved a number of supervised outdoor activities such as camping, fishing, and rock climbing all as part of a genuine wilderness experience. The wilderness around Sheridan was an ideal location for this program. Through Hank's positive attitude and consistent encouragement, Jim was able to gain self-confidence and develop a higher level of self-esteem which greatly decreased his level of depression. Although Jim's progress was slow, he eventually was able to leave the Center and live on his own in town. He continued to return for visits to his friends for many years.

Unfortunately, as the recreation therapy team knew, not every patient story was a success. In 1984, Tom Phillips, a 34 year old Marine Corps veteran from Houston, Texas, was court committed to the Sheridan Center's psychiatric unit suffering with delusions and anger issues. He was a Vietnam vet, who, even ten years after his discharge, could not come to terms with the horrible experiences in Vietnam. Several years before coming to Sheridan, he had been diagnosed with Post Traumatic Stress Disorder (PTSD). By the early 1980's, PTSD had been recognized as an anxiety disorder that can develop after exposure to a terrifying event or ordeal in which grave physical harm occurred or was threatened. Traumatic events that may trigger PTSD include violent personal assaults, natural or human-caused disasters, accidents, or military combat. People with PTSD may startle easily, become emotionally numb (especially in relation to people with whom they are close), lose interest in things they used to enjoy, have trouble feeling affectionate, are irritable, and may become more aggressive, or even violent. They avoid situations that remind them of the original incident, and anniversaries of the incident are often very difficult.

Tom was a classic PTSD patient. He had been a security guard for a Boys' School in Worland, Wyoming; but was fired for abusive behavior toward several of the students. Tom had been committed to the same VA facility three times in the past and had always been discharged for various misbehaviors. The District Court judge who committed Tom recognized that he had a severe mental disorder. He also knew that the Wyoming mental health system was extremely overcrowded and understaffed. His only alternative was prison which the judge knew would be certain disaster. As a veteran, Tom kept returning to the Sheridan VA facility. The recreation therapists tried to channel Tom's aggression into sports, but even that proved futile. He was involved in numerous verbal and physical altercations with other members of the patient softball team; and on one occasion beat a fellow patient severely. After the third fight he was again discharged by the psychiatric unit treatment team. He blamed Hank for his discharge and physically attacked him in his recreation office. Hank was not badly injured, but was too compassionate to bring charges against Tom. Somehow Tom managed to avoid prison, but never was able to adjust to society. Tom died in 1988 of a heart attack in Casper, Wyoming, about two years after his last discharge from the Medical Center. No one attended his pauper's funeral. Hank felt heartsick about Tom and wished they had been able to do more to help his troubled soul.

In 1992, Scott and the other therapists came into contact with two patients whose actions ultimately became one of the low points of the Sheridan Medical Center program. Jim Jones and Jeff Cole were two veteran patients from the psychiatric unit. Both had been diagnosed with the severest form of stress disorders and anger issues. The medical staff recognized the two friends' potential for violence, but could not recommend physical constraints as no violent acts had yet occurred. Scott and Hank had tried repeatedly to keep up the two men's interest in the sports program. For a while, Jim played center field for the patient softball team and Jeff played right field. Jim was a 32 year Denver, Colorado native and Jeff, who was 34, was from Colorado Springs. Jim and Jeff had met through their affiliation with gangs in the Denver area. Scott, having become well acquainted

with both men, was hardly surprised when against medical advice; the two men left the Center.
Their exodus from the Center was reported to police authorities; but no word of their whereabouts was heard for several months. Later, Scott learned that while hitchhiking through Montana, Jim and Jeff were picked up by a young girl driving alone near Billings. Scott could only imagine the horror of this young woman when she realized what the two men had in store for her. Jim and Jeff raped and beat her before drowning her in the Yellowstone River.

After the crime they returned to the Sheridan Center believing that they would receive asylum there. Scott was shocked when he looked out of his office window and saw 10 police cars screeching to a halt at the back door of the psychiatric unit. It hadn't taken long for authorities to determine who had committed this horrible crime and to track them back to Sheridan. Jeff and Jim were surprised to realize that the VA could not offer them asylum. They were both convicted of murder and are serving life sentences. Later, Scott and Hank had many discussions of how they might have prevented this tragedy, but in retrospect, they realized that predicting and altering behavior in individuals with such severe psychoses is often just not possible.

Throughout the 1980's and 90's, the recreation program at Sheridan progressed with both ups and downs. The veterans' problems remained similar, but each case required individual attention to capture just the right treatment. Scott, Hank and Lucy had many discussions regarding patient treatment and they always agreed that diverting the veteran's attention from dwelling on wartime experiences was a major key to success. In this way, recreation therapy stood out as a treatment of choice. Physical activity has always proven to be a principal way to combating mental stress and disorders. Scott thought it was amazing how time on the playing field or just being out in the natural environment could have a beneficial impact on some of the most disturbed individuals. Although a few patients responded relatively quickly, most required long periods of attention and nearly continuous behavior reinforcement. The horror of some combat experiences ran deep into the subconscious. Weeks of good progress were often erased in a single moment of stress, or some small reminder of past experiences.

Although the recreation therapy unit's objective was always to achieve results as soon as possible, this didn't always occur. In 1994, Robert Baker arrived in the Sheridan Center. He was a paranoid schizophrenic with dual personalities and anger issues. He had been in and out of various hospitals and treatment facilities for more than 25 years. Bob had been a witness to the Mai Lai massacre of 1968. At that time, 500 American troops were being killed each week. He had seen many of his buddies killed by what they thought were South Vietnamese soldiers, but who were actually NVA or VC posing as friendlies. Bob told Scott about the time that he had been forced to shoot teenage boys who were hurling grenades at American troops. The vision of these boys dying was constantly with him. The doctors had diagnosed Bob with PTSD, but had no luck with traditional medical treatments. After years on drugs, Bob had withdrawn into a nearly impervious shell. Scott was fully aware of his PTSD diagnosis and had become as much of a confidant as Bob ever allowed. Although conversations with him were few, he occasionally shared his nightmares with Scott. These conversations usually took place as they sat alone during off-station recreational trips out in the Wyoming forest. Scott found out over time that upon his return from Vietnam, Bob found that he was unable to cope with his day-to-day life in society.

As Bob grew angrier and depressed, these feelings came to a head one night when, after drinking for several hours, he was stopped by a police officer for drunk driving. Bob became so enraged that he ended up killing the officer. An understanding judge saved Bob from prison on the condition that he be confined indefinitely to the VA Hospital. When he first arrived, the staff realized he suffered from isolation syndrome as part of his overall condition. Lucy Martin tried to work one-on-one with Bob for several months. She helped Bob participate in the "ropes" program, a type of physical fitness challenge course developed by the recreation therapy department. Each "ropes" participant was part of a ten man team. The idea was to force each patient out of his position of isolation. After months of coaxing and attention from Lucy, Bob was able to participate as a team member. His social skills never really developed fully, but at least he

"Ropes" Physical Fitness Course

was able to make some progress and occasionally socialize with other patients.

The therapy team put a lot of time and effort into cases like Bob's. In one sense, there was a feeling of frustration, knowing that Bob could never truly "get better" and leave the facility. Yet, there was also some belief that a little good could come from their efforts. In the confines of the medical center Bob could at least function on some limited basis. His world consisted of the psychiatric building and several acres of surrounding grounds. Bob was a living example of the long-term effects of war. He had no visitors. His family, if he still had one, made no attempt to see him. His fellow patients and the staff were his only contact with reality. Scott often wondered what would have been Bob's place in life if only he had been spared those few awful days so long ago. When Scott retired from the Center years later, Bob Baker was still there.

Some patients provided the recreation staff with a bit of a break from the hard-core PTSD victims. In 1997, an African-American from Denver, Colorado, committed himself to the Sheridan Center. Although his real name was in the VA records, he was known to patients and staff alike simply as C. J. No one knew what the initials stood for and C. J. was not about to share that secret. C. J. was 35 years old with a long history of alcohol and drug abuse. He had completed his third VA alcohol treatment program. Because he was very friendly and personable with the patients and staff, everyone seemed to be fond of him. It was a running joke about the number of times he had been through the alcohol treatment program. One day he told Scott that he had no intention of stopping his drinking, but that he truly appreciated everyone's concern. He was very active in the recreation therapy program and the recreation staff soon realized that he was very knowledgeable about their activities. They put him in the Intensive Therapy Program. As this was an incentive program where selected patients were paid a small salary to help the staff, C. J. was very successful. He liked getting paid just for talking. The other veterans seemed to look up to him which helped in the success of their treatments. He also helped with off-station activities, assisting the staff in monitoring patient groups on these trips. He had a great sense of humor which made these trips a lot of fun.

C. J. was a Vietnam vet who dealt with his PTSD by staying active without being under the pressure of holding down a normal job. He needed to stay busy in order to keep from back sliding with his alcohol program. He had been in the Army for four years during the 1960's spending one year in Vietnam and three years in the stockade. Scott learned that C. J. had received several high level combat citations, but he never mentioned those. Somehow, C. J. had managed to receive an honorable discharge so he was eligible for veteran's benefits. Scott marveled at Army inefficiency. Unlike many others, he would often talk to other veterans about his military experiences. Scott realized this was a form of therapy both for C. J. and his attentive audiences.

C. J. left the program after completing the 90 day Alcohol/Drug Treatment program. He returned to Denver to be with his family. He had one daughter. Scott often prayed for him to stay straight for his daughter's sake and also for himself. After C.J. graduated, Scott received several cards from him. He was doing well with a job at a grocery store. It was a great pleasure working with him and seeing the progress he made toward a successful future. In one letter, C. J. told Scott he would be "coming home" to the Center soon as he was tired of work and wanted to get back to his friends. He thought a two or three day drinking binge would certainly get him a trip back to Sheridan. Scott laughed when he read C. J.'s note. He knew that C. J. had really mastered the system.

There were very few female veterans between 1972 and 1985 at the Sheridan VA. Because of the lower numbers of females in the military, the medical center had not felt the need to develop female facilities. However, as more female veterans were admitted to the system nationwide, the Sheridan Center recognized the necessity for change. This presented a whole new challenge for the staff. It changed the scope of therapy in a positive direction toward discovering two different aspects of recreation therapy in Mental Health. It was a wonderful advancement and produced many more activities including co-educational softball, volleyball and tennis programs. It brought the two genders closer through greater sportsmanship and respect for the opposite sex. The appearance of the female veterans produced a positive attitude toward the recreation therapy programs as male patients seemed more willing to participate in activities that were co-ed.

Female vets had two major obstacles to overcome. The first was that many had been abused at home and during their military service. Scott could relate with some of these deep seated feeling because of the physical and verbal abuse that he himself had experienced as a child.

Scott had always felt a special affinity with victims of any type of abuse. The second obstacle was that these female vets were continually forced to adjust to a man's world in the military. They were often expected to perform at an equal level physically. Scott remembered the women he met in the military usually exceeded all expectations in their military service. The recreation staff quickly realized that Lucy Martin had great instincts when it came to working with these women. Scott and Hank thought it must have something to do with the theory that, as the book says, "Women are from Venus, Men are from Mars."

Although she experienced great success while working with the female vets, two episodes provided lofty challenges for her skills. Ann Bollinger, a very attractive vet from Florida, had a fondness for sitting on the laps of male patients. Lucy found herself continuously discussing concepts of "boundaries" and "personal space." Teresa, a veteran from Billings, Montana, was observed running from a counselor's office screaming "rape." The counselors at the VA always kept their office doors open for this very reason, but the experience was a glaring reminder of the need for specific treatment services for females versus males. Because of the relationship that Lucy was able to establish with Teresa through her "My Buddies" program, Lucy was able to discover that Teresa had a history of this type of behavior. Lucy was able to provide some insight to the treatment team which enabled them to provide more effective intervention techniques.

After over thirty years in the Sheridan Medical Center recreation unit, Scott was not totally satisfied with the many recreation program changes that occurred after the turn of the century. In 1972, when he arrived, there were 600 resident patients at the Sheridan Veterans Administration Hospital. Scott and the others had spent years building programs and learning what worked and what didn't, largely through trial and error. Throughout these years, they had developed a high degree of confidence in the ability of their programs to get results in improving the patients' physical and social well being, even in some of the most severe cases. By 2005, however, there were only 125 patients resident at the Sheridan facility. Most recreation programs had been subjected to Federal budget cuts. Programs such as the metal shop, wood shop, leather shop, golf course, bowling alley, and 80% of the off-station activities were shut down. As he completed his career, Scott had mixed feelings as to whether these changes were in the best interest of the veterans the Agency had been set up to serve. While he knew that he and his fellow staff had always tried to give a personal touch to each and every patient, he realized that changing methods, funding reductions and an increasing veteran population was bound to have a telling impact on the VA system he had known. He continues to believe that every American veteran with military-related problems, whether physical or mental, deserves the best possible therapeutic assistance. Even today, after several years of retirement, Scott still asks himself if the VA system has evolved for better or worse.

Chapter 4

"Support the Troops." How many times over the past years had Scott heard that phrase? Yet, virtually no one associated that common sentiment with "Support the Veterans." Scott and his fellow recreation staff colleagues at the Sheridan VA Medical Center knew full well, that outside of their families, and sometimes not even then, many veterans fall beyond the scope of the average citizen's concern. It was certainly true in Sheridan where the VA Center was one of the biggest contributors to the local economy, but in terms of the interaction with the community, the Center's patient population might as well be on the moon. To help begin the process of gradually reintroducing their patients into some form of community life, Hank and Scott developed a program for off-station recreational activities. They felt that this was a vital part of the holistic approach to treatment, particularly for psychological cases.

For most of its history, treatment of mental health issues in the VA hospital system had not progressed substantially since the 19th century. Treatments focused largely on physically restraining the patient—for his own good, of course; sedentary activities such as board games, making baskets or developing artistic skills-painting or clay sculpture; and in extreme cases, so-called medical treatments such as "shock therapy" or lobotomy type surgery. The twentieth century added a wide variety of drug treatments to the medical staff's repertoire, some of which actually were beneficial, but many that merely masked the underlying problems. When Scott arrived at the VA center in 1972, few of the live-in patients were ever likely to return to society.

After the end of the Vietnam War, some significant strides were made in the treatment of the long-term physical and psychological effects of combat. Medical advances in areas such as muscle and bone reconstruction, plastic surgery and greatly improved prosthetic devices, helped many wounded veterans fit back into the civilian work force and their home environments. Psychologically traumatized combat veterans also benefited from new methods for treating the "shell-shock" or "flashback" syndromes. New approaches to recreation therapy were also introduced as part of a more comprehensive range of treatments. At his previous duty station at the Lebanon, Pennsylvania VA hospital, Hank had helped develop an off-station element of the recreation program. This involved allowing groups of patients to leave the hospital grounds under supervision for different types of recreational activities.

At first, the hospital administrators were opposed to such programs. Letting patients outside the confines of the institutional grounds was, in some minds, a formula for disaster. Think of the consequences of a patient injuring himself, or others, or even heading for parts unknown. Of course, the potential for negative reaction on the part of the local citizens was another source of difficulty. Administrators were very conscious of negative public relations. Historically, hospital directors were mainstays of the Sheridan business club and social circuit; with the tacit understanding that patients, especially those from psychiatric wards, would be kept a long "arms-length" from ordinary citizens.

From the first, Scott was enthusiastic about Hank's ideas for off-station activities. He realized this concept opened up a whole new dimension of therapy well beyond the limitations of the hospital's restrictive environment. Through a long campaign of pleading, negotiation and creative promises, Scott and Hank finally obtained management's permission to begin a few sojourns outside the grounds. Scott knew there were risks, but he believed the benefits for the patients merited taking a few chances. Unlike regular "civilian" hospitals, VA Medical Centers are literally home to many of the resident patients. Many of the veterans are there for "life." They have often been forgotten by friends and even family members, who cannot deal with their loved one's erratic behaviors. For other veterans, the hospital is a safe haven from the pressures of the outside world. Even though some veterans are medically fit to leave the sanctuary of the institution, many return again to a placc they can call home. The hospital staff and the recreation therapists in particular, often become substitute family for these forgotten souls.

The newly approved off-station activities allowed Scott and his fellow therapists to bring some normal days to the usual monotony of hospital life. As Hank had the most experience in this type of program he naturally took the lead in selecting and organizing the trips outside the hospital grounds. At first, Scott and Lucy went along with Hank and his charges on brief visits to local parks, sports fields and historical sites. These were considered "safe" trips as the veterans could be more easily watched and supervised as the need arose. After awhile, Scott learned the basic tricks of "herding cats" as Hank described his approach to managing an off-site expedition. Scott's first few trips were interesting to say the least, and he soon found out that each time out was a new adventure and that Murphy's Law—"If something can go wrong, it will!" could always be counted on to appear at the most inopportune moment.

Sheridan College Auditorium

One of the first off-station trips Scott led on his own was to a basketball game at the local Sheridan Junior College. Fifteen veterans sat in the stands as a group. Before the beginning of the game it was customary for the announcer to recognize any fans who had come to the game as part of an organized outing. After the usual Rotarians and American Legionnaires were recognized, Scott allowed himself to believe that this just might go OK. But then, the announcer called out, "We would like to welcome the veterans from the Sheridan VA Medical Center." Suddenly the crowd grew quiet and the town fans nearest Scott and his charges noticeably began to edge away from the small group of patients. Among the locals, the VA patients were somewhat of a mystery. Everyone knew they were up there at the "Fort" but having them sitting side by side with "regular" folk was a new experience. Scott began to doubt whether this get-together idea was as smart as it seemed back in the office. Fortunately, the announcer defused any immediate problem by introducing the opposing players and coaches and the citizens' attention was diverted at least for a little while.

For the first quarter, everything was fine as Scott managed to get his group focused on soft drinks and popcorn. One of the patients was a huge man everyone called "Big Mark." Scott had known he was taking a chance by including Big Mark in the excursion. Mark had been in Vietnam with the Marines. He was about six feet, eight inches tall and 350 pounds. Scott wondered how Mark had gotten around the Marine Corps' height and weight restrictions for a combat infantryman. In any case, Mark had suffered terrible experiences in the War and was never able to readjust to life at home. Soon after his return to Wyoming he had been stopped by a highway patrolman for a minor traffic violation. Mark's temper had flared and in the ensuing altercation, Mark had severely injured the policeman. This chance encounter led to Mark being declared incompetent by an expert witness at his hearing. To avoid commitment to the state mental hospital, his family made arrangements to place Mark into the VA hospital system where it was likely he would remain. He was a simple country boy who never should have seen the atrocities of combat. Normally Mark was gentle and quiet, but he had a short fuse that was easily ignited by verbal pressure and loud noise. Scott realized later that the idea of Mark sitting quietly and watching the game was probably a non-starter from the first.

At the end of the first quarter he got into a verbal argument with several of the players from the opposing team. This got the Sheridan student cheering section all excited and they and the rest of the mostly home-team crowd began rooting Mark on. Scott yelled at Mark to sit down and be quiet, but that time was passed. By now the crowd was more interested in the sideline arguments than the game. As the noise level rose and the taunts became more pointed, Mark became more and more agitated. He stood up once more to bring down fury on the opposing team and some in the crowd were reminded of the story of David and Goliath with Mark being Goliath and the entire opposing team playing an out-matched David. As Sheridan was behind at the time, the home fans continued to cheer Mark on even more, hoping to torment the opposing team. And in fact, the strategy seemed to be working. The more distracted the rival team became, the more momentum Sheridan gained. Finally, as regular play time ended with the score tied, the Sheridan coach screamed at Scott, "Can you bring him back at the end of overtime?" The coach could see the referees moving toward a technical foul or even a game forfeit as the home team bears most of the responsibility for an unruly crowd. Scott decided that it was time to get Mark out of the gymnasium and back to the security of the VA as quickly as possible.

On their way out, for some reason, Mark decided that he wanted the game ball. He walked out on the court and demanded the ball from the player who was shooting a free shot during the overtime. Like any smart college scholar, the player nervously handed over the ball. Nobody knew what to do including the referee! As the crowd looked at Scott to see how he was going to handle the situation, Scott was thinking, "Do I want to get my butt kicked in front of three thousand people?" Scott yelled from the sideline, in a firm but commanding voice, "Mark, give him back the ball." Mark turned to Scott and looked at him like King Kong glaring at the approaching aircraft. Scott hoped the many hours he had spent listening sympathetically to Mark's many problems would pay off in this situation. Scott had treated Mark with respect and he believed he had earned the big man's trust. After several tense moments, Mark replied in a voice that sounded something like it could have come from a nervous grizzly bear, "Okay, Scott." Scott never knew what he would have done if Mark had refused to return the ball. The incident changed the momentum of the game once again and at the game's conclusion, the Sheridan team once again found themselves on the losing end. Coach Bart Hastings, a neighbor of Scott's, never let him forget that loss.

A few weeks later, Scott had put the near disaster of the basketball game out of his mind and took the same group to a country western concert. As is common in most small towns in the Mountain West, there was no regular community auditorium so the program was held in the local high school auditorium. The main attraction of the evening was a country and western ballad singer named Jim Ed Brown. He had been high on the country music charts in the 1960's, but in later years was more likely to play small venues in out-of-the-way spots like Sheridan. Once again Big Mark was part of the veteran's group. He had been given strict instructions to stay at Scott's side at all times and to be on his best behavior. Scott positioned his gang in the upstairs balcony to put some space between them and the show.

About a third of the way through the concert Jim Ed developed a cough. As the singer's problem became worse, nearly everyone in the audience wished they could help out with a glass of water or some remedy. While the entire audience focused on the music, Mark told Scott that he needed to use the bathroom. Scott was distracted by the breaking of Jim Ed's voice and didn't think twice about Mark's request. But, as Scott looked over the railing around the balcony, he was shocked to see Mark walking down the center aisle, through the crowd below and directly toward the stage. Scott was certain that some security person would stop Mark before he reached the stage. But the sight of the giant moving toward the singer evidently caused a lapse in the security team's dedication to duty and as Scott watched in dismay, he saw Mark walk right up to Jim Ed. The singer stood as still as a fencepost probably wondering if this was his last song. At the same time, several of the townspeople who must have been at the basketball game the month before realized they had seen this episode play out before, began looking in Scott's direction and imploring him to do something. Scott's first thought was to race down the stairs at the back of the auditorium in an effort to head off Big Mark. Of course, Scott had not a clue what Big Mark was up to. He didn't know if he was going to strangle Jim Ed or ask for his autograph. Either was a distinct possibility. After a few moments, relief washed over Scott as he saw Mark reach into his pocket, retrieve a cough drop and hand it to the singer. Somewhere deep in this troubled man's soul, from the same man that had injured the highway patrolman; was the compassion give Jim Ed a cough drop to relieve his discomfort. Scott arrived on the stage just ahead of four security guards in time to hear Jim Ed thank Mark for his kind gesture. They led Mark back to his seat and the concert went on.

Scott, Hank and Lucy spent many hours discussing the happenings of their off-station trips. Nearly always, some event would occur that pointed out just how far from normal society these veterans had drifted. Simple behaviors that are common on the outside become social barriers for men who are confined in an institutional environment and have sometimes forgotten the ways of the world. The debate between keeping society "safe" from these individuals and taking a chance that contact with the outside just might help their condition was not an easily resolved issue. To Scott it seemed particularly tragic that these men who had given so much for their country should now be largely put away and forgotten by that same nation.

After the experiences of the basketball game and the concert, Scott was leery of leaving the VA Center grounds with his group, but he recognized the benefits of these escapes "to" reality on his patients' lives. Gradually, as the hospital medical staff recognized the positive impacts of these trips on patient behavior, it became easier to get permission for even more adventuresome excursions.

Scott and one of the psychiatric nurses, Rosie Trueblood, had spent nearly two months planning a trip for some of their most chronic psychiatric patients. The trip would be to the Buffalo Bill Museum in Cody, Wyoming, The museum houses collections that interpret the history of Native American culture, the American cowboy, dude ranching, Western conservation, frontier entrepreneurship and, perhaps most importantly, the sources of many of our concepts about the West. Of course, for most psychiatric patients, this was principally a way of escaping the boredom and the physical confines of the hospital. The lore of the Wild West was far from their thoughts.

William F. "Buffalo Bill" Cody

The Cody Museum was 150 miles from Sheridan over Granite Pass, elevation 9,033 feet, and through Shell Canyon, a narrow and winding road, that could be treacherous in the winter. However, it was late spring and the weather forecast was good. Scott decided they would leave at 7:00 in the morning and return to the VA by 4:00 that afternoon. Rosie was bringing all of the patient medications that would be necessary for the day, but they needed to be back to the hospital not later than 6:00 for the next round of meds. Some of these patients simply could not miss their regular treatment without severe reaction.

It began as an absolutely perfect day. The trip through the mountains was uneventful and the scenery beautiful. Although the patients were outside of their normal, protective environment, there seemed to be a feeling of contentment mixed with anticipation. Scott and Rosie had no idea of the ordeal that lay ahead. They arrived in Cody about 11:00 in the morning and decided to have lunch at the local Holiday Inn restaurant before going on to the museum. Because it was nearing lunch hour, the restaurant was full to capacity and Rosie realized that this might be a problem for several patients including Kevin Briggs who suffered from extreme paranoia. She and Scott seated Kevin at a table by himself and then found seats for the rest of the group. They were all enjoying their meals when out of nowhere Kevin suddenly erupted like a volcano. He stood up on his chair and to the amazement of all the customers screamed, "Let me out of here, you bastards!" This outburst sent some customers scrambling for the door but most simply sat at their tables in shock waiting for the next outburst. Fortunately, Scott kept his cool and calmly walked Kevin out to the van for a cigarette. In a few minutes Kevin had forgotten why he was mad. His mood swings went as quickly as they came. Rosie remained to calm the rest of the group and to try to explain things to the manager in an effort to avoid a call to the local police.

After the fiasco in the restaurant, the veterans finally arrived at the museum. Kevin decided to remain in the van for which Scott was highly grateful. Of course, putting Kevin in the van and keeping him there were two different things. Scott and Rosie did their best to keep the group together and moving, but they realized that nearly anything could set off a chain reaction. After about 30 minutes, Scott was shocked as he saw Kevin running through the museum. Scott began chasing him to prevent him from knocking over any of the priceless Frederick Remington bronze sculptures. The whole time he was thinking, "How would he be able to explain this to the VA director." "Sorry, but you owe the Buffalo Bill Museum $500,000 in damages!" Fortunately, Scott was able to restrain Kevin before security threw them all out. Of course, within minutes Kevin had forgotten the entire episode and was busy counting the cars in the parking lot. Scott's feeling of relief was short lived as he spotted Harold Keys, another patient, approaching a security guard. Harold was a strange looking patient who called everyone "Dear." He asked the guard, "Smoke in here, Dear? Smoke in here, Dear? Smoke in here, Dear?" as he tossed cigarettes out of his pocket and onto the marble floor. The guard responded in an angry voice, "No, you can't smoke here and quit calling me Dear!" as he watched cigarettes flying everywhere.

This latest social blunder pretty well sealed the fate of the museum visit. The museum manager advised Scott to remove his charges at once and that he would be pleased if they never set foot on museum property again. Scott and Rosie didn't argue. They could see the manager's point. Feeling as if they had been in a street fight, Scott and Rosie decided that it was time to head back to Sheridan. As they left Cody, they soon realized that miscues from the weather forecasters were about to add even more chaos to this nightmare. Snow was beginning to fall and they weren't even to the worst portion of the road. The snow began in earnest as they left Shell Canyon and began the long grade up Granite Pass. By now they were experiencing the full effects of one of those freakish Wyoming spring snowstorms.

It quickly became evident that the group would not be able to make it to the hospital by the 6:00 medication time. As darkness came on, Scott and Rosie noticed an increasingly higher level of anxiety and nervousness in the patients. Rosie had administered the last of her medications an hour or two before and some of the patients were really getting restless. She suggested they might stop and spend the night at Arrowhead Lodge at the top of Granite Pass, still 60 miles from Sheridan. Scott thought of the prospect of spending the night in a room with 6 un-medicated psychiatric patients who were approaching near panic or continuing through a blinding snowstorm, Scott chose to forge ahead. Things got worse and a minor fight broke out between Kevin and Jerry Walters, another difficult paranoiac. Scott was trying to help Rosie settle the men down and drive at the same time. It didn't work. He hit a patch of ice and lost control of the van for just a moment. That's all it took. The road shoulder was soft from the snow and ice and the wheels dug in as they left the pavement. Scott managed to stop but he knew the spinning tires meant they were stuck. This was not a good situation. He knew that any sensible drivers were already home by the fire. There was a possibility that the highway patrol was out, but there were few of them in this area. Scott picked out the three calmest patients and got them positioned behind the van to push as he tried to gently rock the vehicle out of the mud and snow. It took a lot of luck and more than a little skill, but Scott managed to get them back on the pavement. Everyone was cold, wet and irritated, but needless to say when they finally made it back after midnight, the lights of Sheridan had never looked better.

The great Museum trip, as it became known as later, was Scott's last off-station trip that ventured more than 50 miles from the Center. Certainly, it was his last one if there was any possibility of snow.

Unlike the patients in a regular community hospital, the staff at the VA Medical Center not only had to provide for their charges medical needs, but also create a permanent living environment for each veteran that, at least in part, mirrored the outside society. The days in the wards were long and tedious. Many of the patient groups, particularly in the alcoholic, drug, and geriatric sections, were going to be in residence for long periods of time. Under these circumstances it fell to the recreation therapy team to develop activities to help make the time pass more enjoyably or at least to give some opportunity to break the boredom. Sheridan is very cold in the winter so most patient activities had to occur indoors. The therapists found that there were only so many games you could play and TV programs to watch before the patients became increasingly restless and in extreme cases even violent.

Everyone looked forward to the first warm spring day when the picnic season could begin. Scott found that regular picnic trips not only helped take up a lot of time, but were a major part of the therapeutic program. Also, a picnic was the type of activity where the largest number of patients could participate. Usually Scott and the other therapists took about 70 patients with 2 to 3 staff members to help supervise. Most often, two busses were loaded with picnickers and all of the food and equipment necessary for 70+ people. The area around Sheridan is a paradise for outdoor activities. For many years the picnics were held at Pine Island, a beautiful rustic camping area in the Big Horn Mountains about 40 miles from Sheridan. Goose Creek ran beside the picnic area and made the location a nice place for the day's outing. The area had a pavilion, tables, fire grills and horseshoe pits. Scott and the patients even built a makeshift softball field and volleyball court. Best of all, the area was far enough from town that it was virtually deserted during the week. Scott had realized that his group didn't always mix well with "real" folks. It was Scott's responsibility to build the fires, cook and oversee the picnic itself. Often he assigned jobs to the more responsible patients. This made them feel more at home and seemed to be good therapy. Some of the patients always seemed eager to help with the cooking, games, and even the clean up. They felt a sense of accomplishment at being a useful part of the group.

As great an activity as the picnic outings were, the recreation therapy staff always had to be on the lookout for trouble. Some of the patients, particularly from the geriatric unit had a habit of heading for the tall timber on any occasion. Once an 80 year-old patient wandered away from the group and was lost in the woods for 6 hours. Scott was afraid that the old man might never be found. When he was finally found he was frightened and delusional. Scott soon learned that it was good practice to pair up each patient with one or two others. In this way they seemed to somehow watch after each other. Although it was strictly against hospital rules, Scott sometimes tied particularly restless patients to a tree to keep them from wandering too far. Scott would tie about a 30 foot piece of clothesline to the tree and the other end around the patient's leg. This seemed to work well. Scott always wondered why none of the patients ever thought to untie the rope.

Once in a while, patient disappearances became more serious. After enjoying a particularly beautiful day in the mountains, the busses had been loaded for the return trip to the VA. After the headcount, Scott realized one patient was missing. A frantic search of the area failed to discover the missing man. The Center security office was notified and the State Search and Rescue team was called to aid in the search. Scott knew that even in springtime, night in the mountains could be cold and treacherous. The woods are as dark as a coal mine after sunset and the temperature can easily drop below freezing. Hypothermia was a real danger to anyone spending a night in the wilderness. After another eight hours of searching the man finally appeared at midnight at the front gate of the hospital demanding to be let in. He had somehow traveled the 40 miles from the picnic grounds to home. Questioning by security resulted in no answers. The patient had no idea how he made it home, but was certainly happy to be there. The staff speculated he had hitched a ride back to Sheridan. Afterwards, Scott could hardly describe the feeling of panic that he had felt knowing that he had lost a patient in the mountains and the relief he felt when he learned that the man had been found.

Some of the incidents involving runaway patients did not end happily. In one case, the picnic area at Pine Island was the scene of a real tragedy. Patients and staff had enjoyed another day in the beautiful mountains and were on the bus and ready to leave the area. One of the patients asked the bus driver if he could have one last cigarette before the trip back to Sheridan. For smokers this was important as the hospital did not permit smoking on the bus. When the bus driver opened the door, a second patient jumped off the bus and ran for Goose Creek. Before anyone could stop him he had done a swan dive into the freezing water. The creek was high and very swift with the spring runoff. Henry Blake, one of the recreation therapists, along with two nurses, jumped in the water to rescue him, but the swift water had already carried him too far down stream. Henry did not know how to swim so it took great courage on his part to even attempt the rescue. The patient's death was ruled a suicide, but the entire staff was devastated at their inability to save him. After that incident, all geriatric picnics were held on-station.

Goose Creek at Pine Island

Another favorite location for picnics was at the city park in the nearby town of Story. This was a favorite location for some because they had an opportunity while on the picnic to take swimming lessons at the community pool. This activity was particularly good for the alcohol and drug patients as they yearned for any diversion to keep their minds off their addictions. During one of these lessons, the instructor had the group line up in the shallow end of the pool. As might be expected, one of the patients headed into the deep end and had to be rescued by the instructor during the first 5 minutes of the class. Later, Scott noticed a pair of swimming trunks floating on the water. He told everyone to stay in the water until the swim suit was matched to its owner. Fortunately there were no ladies present except the nurses who had seen everything imaginable.

Story, Wyoming, Picnic Pavilion and Sports Field

Once, Scott had taken a group to Story for a picnic. The staff noticed that one of the patients and his dog were missing. After a frantic search, they were found together going down the water slide at the park swimming pool. Scott had a difficult time explaining to the life guard that in the patient's mind that was a perfectly normal thing to do.

Confinement in the alcoholic unit was particularly difficult for those patients. Generally they were there voluntarily to try to beat their problem. The VA policy was that there was no second chance at the facility for falling off the wagon. In later years, as cost reduction programs reduced the number of alcohol and drug abusers that could be in residence, toleration for alcohol-related patients was negligible. On another picnic in Buffalo, two alcoholic patients turned up missing. Scott and a nurse finally found them in a bar in town. Scott never forgot the look on their faces when they were caught drinking. They realized that another chance to beat their habit was lost. The two men were discharged from the hospital later that day. The "zero tolerance" policy was tough, but it was the only practical way to deal with recurring alcohol and drug users.

One advantage of having a veteran's facility in Sheridan was that the surrounding countryside provided a perfect setting for Hank's "Nature Awareness" program. The area provided countless opportunities to observe nature up close. Many of the patients were city boys whose idea of wildlife was a flock of pigeons in a city park. Hank was the perfect person to introduce these guys to a world they knew little about, but that could be fascinating to anyone who needed daily changes from the sameness of the hospital. One of Hank's academic degrees was in horticulture. He was a walking encyclopedia when it came to trees and other vegetation. His expertise also included the wildlife of Wyoming including bear, elk, birds and any number of woodland creatures. Once a week, Hank would schedule a nature trip for one of the alcohol, psychiatric, Alzheimer's, or geriatric units. Because the administrators would allow only 10 patients at a time on the nature trips, there was some real competition to earn a spot. Hank and Scott used this desire to get out of the wards to help control patient behavior. It was strictly a carrot-stick approach, but everyone knew that just a small infraction of the rules would move your name lower on the roster of those scheduled for the next outing. The patients even helped enforce the rules by reporting even the smallest misbehavior. There was no peer loyalty when it came to getting an extra privilege.

Hank remembered with great fondness the story of one particular nature trip. He had spotted a large elk herd in the Big Horn mountains close enough to the road to permit close-up viewing with only a short hike from the bus. Hank announced that this day's trip was to be special and the 10 selected to go were to be on their best behavior. Hank made it clear several times that everyone must be very quiet to approach within several hundred yards of the herd. All the patients had done pretty well in maintaining silence as they tromped through the woods. When they stopped at the edge of the clearing they could see 40 or 50 of the magnificent creatures grazing on the mountain grasses.

As they took turns viewing through the binoculars, Hank overheard one veteran ask another, "Is that an elk?"

"Yes, it's a cow," another replied.

"But, I thought you said it was an elk!" The first responded.

Another man spoke out, "I think it's a bull!"

To this, the first man screamed aloud, "I thought you said it was an elk!"

"Bull" or "Cow" Elk?

By now the entire herd was disappearing over the far hill, and Hank couldn't help but laugh out loud. He thought to himself that his group had a way-to-go in their study of wildlife, but he knew that for most of these men just seeing these animals in the wild was a real thrill. Whenever Hank recalled this story, it reminded him of the simple pleasures that can raise the spirits of men for whom life held so little enjoyment.

One of Scott's favorite stories about these nature trips was the time that he had taken 30 year old Jim Smith on Sheridan's City Walking Tour. Sheridan is not a large town, but to the veterans, any chance to walk in the open air away from the Center really was a special time. Jim was one of those borderline patients who just might have a chance in regular society if he could control his emotional outbursts. Scott encouraged him to talk about his plans for the future. He realized that just the ability to envision a future outside the institution was something unusual among many of the patients. The subject that day was good places for retirement. Jim had thoughts of some day living in a nice warm climate, with little or no worries, sitting on the porch just watching the people pass by. Scott mentioned that his own father was retired and living in San Miguel de Allende near Mexico City. The small Mexican town had an expatriate community of about 600 people from around the world and great weather for tennis and other outdoor activities.

About a month after this discussion, Jim was discharged from the VA Center. The doctors were hoping that he could re-adjust to the outside world. Six weeks later, Jim showed up in San Miguel. He was drunk and went to the favorite local cantina looking for John Reemers, saying that he was Scott's best friend from Sheridan, Wyoming. Scott's Dad, John, often reminded Scott of the strange visitor who had surprised him that day in San Miguel. The follow-up investigation revealed that Jim actually had no family of his own and no place to go, and soon after, Scott lost track of Jim. He hoped that the man had found some place to call home. The fact that the man traveled 3,000 miles to visit the father of his therapist indicated to Scott just how lonely a person can become.

In addition to the antics of the patients, the off-station programs also provided some experiences for the staff. Scott and a nurse had taken his recreation re-socialization group for a tour of the local YMCA. When the tour guide got to the locker room, he failed to mention that it was a men's only area. So the nurse followed the group right in. After awkward stares and a few remarks from numerous unclad men, she was in such a panic to escape from this embarrassing situation that she could not find the door to get out. To this day, the boys around the YMCA still recall the woman in the men's locker room and wonder when and if that nurse is coming back! It's a very small town.

Sheridan YMCA

During his years at the VA, Scott and the other therapists experienced a number of frightening and traumatic moments. In May, 1979, Scott was having coffee and chatting with Mary Heath who was the VA telephone operator. At that time, the telephone office, admissions, and the security office were side-by-side. There was a Dutch door between the phone office and admissions. Suddenly, Mary looked up at Scott with fear in her eyes. "What's wrong?" he whispered.

She replied under her breath, "A patient has a pistol pointed at the head of Dan, the admissions officer." The patient could see Mary, but he could not see Scott, who quietly told her to call the security officer who was next door.

An ex-Denver city cop, Mike Benson, the officer on duty, knew he needed to keep the situation calm, so he did not come in with his gun drawn. Instead he did an excellent job of talking the veteran into putting down the gun and returning to the ward. Without a doubt Mike saved Dan's life. Scott told Mary that if the gunman would have shot Dan, the two of them would have gone out the window. Later, Scott asked Dan if he had been nervous. He said, "No, but that bullet would have made a bigger hole going out than going in!" The security officer got a well-deserved award for his actions. The patient had somehow smuggled the gun into his area some time before. Even after questioning, he really couldn't explain his actions. He told the resident psychiatrist he had just been angry over some trivial incident.

Another night that stuck in Scott's mind was an evening in October, 1998. One of the most popular nurses with the patients was a dedicated lady named Mary Slater. She was sitting at her nurses' station that evening on the psychiatric unit. Things had been very quiet, but when she looked up at the door, she was facing a distraught patient with a 357 magnum pointed straight at her head! Mary screamed and the man fired the pistol. The bullet missed her head by only inches! The shock of actually firing the gun seemed to bring the man back to reality. He threw the weapon to the floor and ran into the night. The police found him later cowering in a ditch behind the unit and arrested him. Mary never fully recovered from that moment of terror. She had to take an entire year off before she could face returning to work.

One can only imagine the tormented thoughts that brought this veteran to the point of firing a pistol at an innocent person. These incidents involving the potential of death brought home to Scott just how disturbed some of these patients were and how violence was often in check just below the surface. He recalled his own days in combat and could easily understand how those experiences could profoundly impact a person's entire future life.

One case that actually did cross over the line of extreme violence involved Jeff Broomfield, an out-patient who attended the Center's weight training program as well as regular counseling sessions. The doctors felt Jeff was able to live at home with his wife and children despite his frequent bouts of depression. Although he was almost always very friendly and outgoing with the staff, they knew he suffered from PTSD due to his experiences in Vietnam. Jeff was able to share some of these experiences with Hank, who had developed the exercise program for the out-patients as well as patients staying at the facility. Jeff seemed to function well when he was on anti-depressant medication. However, when a medication no longer worked for him or when he failed to take them, he had a tendency toward violence.

During one of these bouts, he became extremely belligerent toward his wife and in an effort to protect her children, she called the police. When the police arrived, Jeff charged them with a knife. Scott and most of the Center staff believed that this confrontation was actually an attempted suicide. The police were forced to shoot him in self-defense. Jeff died on the scene. Scott, Hank, and Lucy attended his funeral. They knew that they would miss this man's smile and sense of humor. As is often the case, they wondered if they could have done something more to prevent this tragedy. It was a good lesson for Scott and the other staff to always remember that every patient was there for a reason and that unexpected behavior could come from any direction.

Tragedies such as these, occurred infrequently, but left a permanent psychological mark on the staff members, were one of the reasons that the recreation staff felt that it was imperative to relate with one another in good humored ways in order to relieve the stress and anxiety. Practical jokes were frequently played on one another. They knew just how therapeutic laughter can be. In fact, comedian, Don Rickles once said, "The world would be a better place if we all learned to laugh at ourselves and one another."

Scott and his partners were always looking for new ways to help the patients cope with everyday life. Lucy had developed two important initiatives, pet therapy and kid therapy programs for her patients on the Geriatric Unit. Regardless of their mental state it is surprising how many patients will respond positively to children and pets. Their reactions are almost instinctive. Lucy's kid therapy program was known as "My Buddies" program. She would ask elementary students to write letters with the patients and to come to the Center for Christmas and Halloween parties. The patients as well as the staff thought it was great fun to watch the children bobbing for apples, unwrapping presents or just listening to Christmas stories. Lucy was a "hugger." She always tried to show her true feelings for her patients through a hug and a good word.

As part of Lucy's pet therapy program, she sometimes had the children and staff members bring their personal pets to interact with the patients. These pets included cats, dogs and on several occasions, Hank even brought in his horses for the patients to ride. The program was very successful and the staff never tired of seeing the pleasure on the faces of the patients. However, the housekeeping service thought Lucy had gone too far when she brought Andean lamas into the elevator and onto the geriatric unit, much to the shock of the unit nurses.

Lucy had planned to include an aquarium in her pet therapy program. She ordered the aquarium and several very expensive tropical fish. She had waited at least 6 weeks for the fish to arrive. On the big day, Scott was the only staff member on duty when the FEDEX truck made its delivery. He was supposed to leave with 16 patients on an off-station trip in 15 minutes and needed to find a place to store the fish until Lucy could add them to their new home. Being a trout fisherman from Colorado, he assumed fish always thrived in cold water. So, he put them in the refrigerator and left to supervise his next activity. Upon Lucy's return, she found her fish belly up. The only comment she made to Scott was, "Does the word tropical mean anything to you?" Scott never lived this story down. It will be on his tombstone, "He murdered tropical fish."

Hank also developed the annual Fun Run, a mini-marathon involving many of the patients and staff members. This was a great opportunity for the entire VA to get together for fun and friendly competition. Participants could walk or run 1 mile, 5 miles, or use a wheel chair for these distances. Ribbons were given to everyone in all classes. It was always rewarding to see the faces of the winners and the inspiration the event gave to everyone who participated. The staff always went through the ritual of an interview for each winner, just to make them feel a little special.

The Recreation Therapy unit was known as the prank department, especially on birthdays. Each person's birthday was a special occasion. One time the staff hired a stripper to come to Scott's bowling league to perform a singing telegram for him. Scott was so surprised and quite embarrassed as she kissed him on the cheek at the end of her performance. To this day he continues to believe that his favorite nurse, Jan Little set the whole thing up. At the anniversary of Scott's 25th year at the Center, his co-workers had Stacy Barton dress up like a "playboy" bunny. She made his 25 years at the VA well worth it. The recreation staff once had Hank come to a phony staff meeting where Betty Howgrate was to bring a cake and give him a big birthday kiss right on the lips. Betty had always been one of Hank's favorite co-workers. He had an innocent crush on her, but he was so bashful when the big moment came, he turned his head and he got the kiss on his cheek instead. He said it was the worst move he had made since playing as linebacker at Penn State. Hank was so nervous that he broke into a cold sweat and Scott had to wipe this giant-of-a-man's forehead. The staff laughed until tears ran down their cheeks.

Lucy was a very attractive woman. So, Hank and Scott never tired of teasing her about the effect she had on men. They would remind her of the fact that they were barely able to get a phone in their office while hers looked like an AT&T warehouse. They laughed as they remembered the time a famous entertainer had come to the VA to perform in a USO show and constantly reminded Lucy's husband about what a lucky man he was. Lucy told the guys that her husband was not amused. Then there was the time that Hank and Lucy had gone to visit the VA Medical Center in Fort Meade, South Dakota. The director of recreation, John Armstrong, was so smitten with Lucy that he forgot most of his presentation and could barely put a sentence together. At lunch he further embarrassed himself by spilling his tray with soup and salad right in front of Lucy. She really felt sorry for the man, but of course Hank and Scott thought it was a great joke.

Scott and Hank teased Lucy about the fact that she could be in recreation and know so little about sports. One special day, Johnny Unitas, the Hall of Fame quarterback for the Baltimore Colts, showed up at the VA unexpectedly. Lucy called Scott at home saying that a man calling himself Johnny Unitas was standing there beside her, but that she had never heard of him and didn't know who he was. After ascertaining that the visitor was truly Unitas, Scott told her to take him over to the drug and alcohol unit because they would certainly know him. Johnny was on a hunting trip to Montana, and because he thought so highly of American Veterans, he wanted to stop by the Sheridan VA Center to shake hands and sign a few autographs. Scott was so envious that he did not get to meet Unitas as he had heard of the great football legend since childhood. He was not surprised that Lucy didn't know Johnny Unitas, seeing that she didn't know anyone else in the National Football League. The alcohol and drug patients really got a thrill from the surprise visit.

In many cases, the Sheridan recreation therapy program provided the only chance at "normalcy" for the veterans at the hospital. Most of the experiences, especially the off-station trips, had a very positive effect on the participants. Scott, Hank and the others saw the few difficulties more as a "lessons learned" experience than a real set-back. Many of the patients would be confined at the Sheridan Center for a large portion of their lives. For those who did leave, the brief contacts with the outside world often helped build a bridge back to reality. For all, patients and staff alike, the ability to enjoy simple pleasures and laugh together became a big part of the total health care experience that these therapists were able to provide to the veterans in their care.

Chapter 5

"By the time we were drafted or enlisted to fight in Vietnam, we had already been indoctrinated for that war since childhood by the mythology of America. One myth we soaked up was "cowboys and Indians" - the long saga telling how white Europeans carved a great nation out of a land inhabited by savages. But when we went to war, it wasn't much like the movies. Not much of a script. The guys in white hats weren't winning, and weren't the good guys anyway. The victims weren't grateful. Death wasn't noble. War was mostly confusing and sometimes terrifying. At best, we survived, hoping to come back alive.

General Custer was on a search-and-destroy mission at Little Big Horn. Not much difference between Wounded Knee and My Lai or between forced relocation to reservations and the resettlement camps we built in Vietnam."

Ben Chitty
Clarence Fitch Chapter
Vietnam Veterans Against the War
April 1998

Wyoming is sometimes known as the Cowboy State. Many people think of cowboys and Indians when they think of Wyoming. In fact, when Scott and Kate visited Washington D.C. for the Bi-Centennial celebration in 1976, they were often asked questions by curious easterners about the Wyoming wilderness and the cowboys and Indians. A few people asked if still they circled up the wagons against Indian attacks.

Cowboys were not the only people to influence the culture and development of Sheridan. Native Americans also played a huge role in the history of the area including the events leading up to Custer's Last Stand at the Little Big Horn. Because of this historical influence, the recreation therapy staff at the Sheridan Medical Center tried to take advantage of the proximity of several historic points of interest in the surrounding area. They often took the veterans on off-station trips to places such as Fort Phil Kearney and Fetterman Battlefield, as well as into Montana to visit the Little Big Horn Battlefield National Monument. Ask anyone what was the longest war in U. S. history. Some will say the Civil War, some World War II, others Viet-Nam. Of course, they're not even close. Since America became independent and began its westward expansion there was nearly a continuous war against Native Americans beginning seriously in the 1830's and continuing until the last pitched battle in Northern Arizona in 1917.

After the Civil War, a western migration overwhelmed the Great Plains with easterners looking for riches, a new life, or in many cases, farms and ranch land. Many miners from the east also came to Wyoming and Montana in search of gold. Much of this land was home to the mighty Sioux nation and other nomadic tribes. Deadly conflicts arose between the miners and settlers and the Native Americans who lived in this territory. The newcomers demanded that the government provide protection and safe passage from these attacks. Three forts were established along the trail to these gold fields.

Leaders like Sitting Bull, Red Cloud and Crazy Horse, chiefs of the Sioux tribe, reacted harshly against these hated forts. On December 21, 1866 Red Cloud's warriors attacked and killed more than 80 soldiers at Fort Phil Kearny near Sheridan. The massacre of William Fetterman and his ill-fated troops ignited a surge of Army presence into the Wyoming Territory. Eventually, because of the relentless attacks by Red Cloud, the US Government abandoned Fort Phil Kearney and the Indians burned the fort to the ground. The fort was partially reconstructed in the early 20th century as a state historical site.

Fort Phil Kearny

Conflicts between Native Americans and white settlers continued, and by the winter of 1876, military officials in Washington D.C. had decreed that the Sioux and their allies, the Northern Cheyenne, move to the reservation or be considered at war with the United States Government. Sitting Bull refused to give in to the American government. He said that he would "die on a good horse, fighting the whites." The Sioux tribe and their leaders only wanted to be left alone on their traditional homeland. Their quest for independence and struggle to remain off the reservation culminated on June 25, 1876, in the battle popularly known as Custer's Last Stand.

Now known as the Battle of the Little Bighorn, this action occurred approximately 70 miles north of Sheridan. The National Park Service has acknowledged both U.S. and Native American military personnel at the site which is now a national cemetery. In 1881, a marble pillar was installed to honor the dead soldiers. Later, a Congressional bill changed the name of the monument and provided an Indian memorial that was built near Last Stand Hill. On Memorial Day of 1991, granite markers were placed on the battlefield where hundreds of Native Americans fell.

The history of the veterans at the Sheridan Medical Center has historically been linked to the development of the city of Sheridan itself. By the early 1930's the small town of Sheridan, Wyoming was so quiet that people said that "you could hear the eagles soaring in the sky."

Sheridan WYO Rodeo Grounds

Some of the local citizens decided that a rodeo might add some excitement to the town and, of course, perhaps generate some business for local merchants. They wanted it to be a professional rodeo that could rival some of the major shows around the country such as Cheyenne Frontier Days. The entire community became involved in the effort.

The Sheridan-WYO-Rodeo was founded to help the Sheridan Community and has continued to do so during its seventy-seven year history. Early rodeos were influenced significantly by William F. (Buffalo Bill) Cody's Wild West Show of the 19th century. That show featured a grand battle between the Army and the Indians that was the highlight of the spectacle. Army veterans, mountain men and real Indians, including Sitting Bull himself, were part of the show. Buffalo Bill Cody auditioned talent for his "Wild West Show" from the porch of the Historic Sheridan Inn.

Historic Sheridan Inn

The first Sheridan rodeo was held in the summer of 1931. Events such as parades, a carnival, and an Indian show helped bring thousands to the tiny town. Rodeo professionals from throughout the United States as well as hundreds of Indians performing in "wild west" shows delighted the spectators. That first Sheridan rodeo was deemed a huge success. Throughout the years many special events involving Native Americans occurred during the rodeo days. In 1932 the Crow and Cheyenne tribes smoked a peace pipe; the first rodeo queen was selected in 1936. In 1951, Sheridan won two national human relations awards after Lucy Yellow Mule, a Crow Indian, was elected rodeo queen by popular applause. Today the Sheridan-WYO Rodeo is one of the premier professional rodeos in the United States.

The recreation therapy staff always looked forward to the events surrounding the rodeo with some measure of trepidation. In theory, the rodeo was an opportunity to relate the wartime events that had shaped the lives of the veterans at the medical center to the history of the local community. In practice, most of the veterans had little knowledge of history and no real interest in any past other than their own. However, all of the patients looked forward to some excitement and relished any opportunity to get away from the daily routine of the wards.

The first event of the several days of celebration was the big parade. Several buses were used to transport patients to downtown Sheridan, where 40 to 50 patients were thrust into a crowd of 40,000 people. The recreation staff was expected to keep track of everyone. This proved to be nearly impossible as, once off the bus, patients scattered like ants at the annual company picnic. Patients from the alcohol unit were often discovered visiting the local "watering holes." A traditional rodeo activity involved several contestants racing antique iron beds on wheels down the main street of town. These "bed" races were held right before the start of the big parade. Scott was frequently terrified to see the beds careening toward the by-standers, some of which were his patients. Usually, no one was hurt, but often the crowds scattered as the beds sped out-of-control toward the finish line.

The Sheridan WYO Rodeo along with the carnival was held each year at the Sheridan Fairgrounds on the west end of town. Through the generosity of the Rodeo Committee, the Medical Center was able to obtain tickets for every patient wishing to attend the rodeo. Of course, nearly everyone wanted to go. Each year, more than 80 patients from all the units (Psychiatric, Alcohol Treatment, Geriatric and Alzheimer's) were once again loaded onto busses and driven to the fairgrounds. They had a special section in which to sit, but keeping the patients in their seats was next to impossible. One always wondered what they would get into next. If Scott and the rest of the staff had a dollar for every patient that they had found at the nearby carnival they could have retired years earlier. The carnival had all the temptations known to man. There were the lights, music, and most of all the girls! Scott likened it to taking kids to a candy store and then telling them that they couldn't go in! The veterans used any excuse to melt into the crowd: looking for refreshments, bathroom runs, better seats, or any of a hundred other ruses. Scott once found a patient dressed up like a clown. He had convinced the rodeo clowns that he wanted to go on the road with them. They laughed when they found out the real story. John Heath was a professional rodeo performer going through the alcohol abuse program. Scott almost had a heart attack when he looked up and saw John on a bronco ready to ride. When John bailed out at the last minute, Scott realized that he could start breathing again.

On a hot day in July, a cool beer was a real treat for the rodeo fans. Naturally the beer vendor always showed up at the wrong time. Henry, one of the recreation therapists, had asked that the vendors not sell beer in the VA section. He was an old time recreation specialist from the days of the locked cells and burly guards. He still believed in lock-downs and physical punishment for errant patients. None of these "modern" therapy methods would do for Henry. Well, that didn't go over very well, so a shouting match developed between Henry and the beer vendor. The salesman knew full well that 80 or so ex-military folks would likely be fine customers with a lot of repeat business. All of the alcohol ward patients were hoping the beer seller would win the argument. In 30 years there was never a rodeo during which at least one patient failed to get thoroughly drunk on beer. On one occasion a psychiatric ward patient had too many beers and by the time it was over he was so belligerent that he refused to get on the bus. The driver threatened to leave him behind, but fortunately, Henry was able to persuade him to join them for the ride home. When he arrived at the VA, he had to be put into restraints. The next morning the patient thanked the staff for a really great day at the rodeo. He was already looking forward to next year.

Before the handicap accessible grandstands were built, the rodeo committee provided a flatbed truck with a ramp from which the wheelchair patients could watch the rodeo. The ramp was a simple wooden plank with no side rails. The ramp had no traction and became very slippery when wet. Marty Stone, a geriatric ward nurse, was taking a wheelchair veteran down the ramp at the close of the performance. Naturally, she had worn her cowboy boots. She began to slide at the top of the ramp and she had no way to stop herself. Marty and the wheelchair patient began to slide quickly down the ramp out of control while others watched their descent in horror. No one thought that it would be possible to get to them in time to prevent the runaway chair from wiping out the crowd at the foot of the ramp. When Hank saw this, the ex-Penn State linebacker, ran as fast as any linebacker has ever run. He grabbed Marty with one hand and the wheelchair cowboy with the other in time to prevent a real catastrophe. His quick thinking and his ability saved the day.

Later that particular rodeo night, Scott was sitting with Lucy when he mistakenly remarked, “Lucy, have you noticed how well things are going at the rodeo tonight?” What a dumb thing to say. At that moment, one of Lucy’s patients walked up the stairs. Blood was gushing from a wound to her head. The woman had been playing one of the games in the carnival when a sudden wind storm came up. A gust had blown the top of the booth down and it had landed on directly on her head. Scott rushed the patient to the hospital emergency room which was across the street from the rodeo grounds. She was diagnosed with a concussion and had an enormous headache. In the meantime, Lucy went back to the carnival to confront the person responsible for her charge’s injuries. After the accident, the man from the carnival had handed the lady a Teddy Bear and sent her on her way without determining just how badly she was injured. Before it was all over, Lucy had the carnival manager, the sheriff, the police department and probably her attorney there and she was chewing everyone's butt for allowing her patient to wander off. For the remainder of his career, Scott never again mentioned to Lucy that things were "going well."

Once the rodeo was over you might think that everyone just got on the bus for the return trip to the Medical Center. Not so! It was a case of "find two—lose one." The recreation staff took nearly an hour to gather up the 80 patients, staff, and volunteers only to find that someone had stolen one of the buses. Later it was discovered that some high school kids had taken it on a joy ride around town. The staff struggled to keep everyone together while they were forced to wait for another bus to arrive from the Center. Tempers frayed, but finally, substitute transportation arrived. After that experience Scott told Hank how thankful he was that rodeo week occurred only once a year.

Another local celebration to honor the influence of Native American culture on the area was the All American Indian Days Rodeo and Celebration held in Sheridan each summer. Most of the Native American tribes in the United States were represented at the event. The Miss Indian America pageant was a part of the festivities. One of the volunteer duties of the hospital staff was to honor the pageant participants by escorting them to breakfast on the first day of the celebration. A male hospital staff member was paired with each candidate. Hank and Scott were anxious to discover with whom they would be paired. Hank was pleased to learn that he was to escort a very pretty Cherokee woman from

Oklahoma. However, Scott ended up spending the morning with a very angry candidate from Montana. Not only was the young lady lacking in physical charms, she seemed determine to punish Scott for all of the injustices suffered by the Native Americans beginning with the landing of Columbus 500 years earlier. Throughout the entire breakfast, she continued to harass him about the fact that his relatives had stolen the land of her people. All Scott knew was that his family was an Irish clan from Ohio that had migrated to America long after the last Indian uprising. It didn't take long for Scott to realize he was in a no-win situation with the Montana representative. By then he just wanted the whole morning to end as soon as possible. Much later, he was able to laugh about the incident with the "beauty" from Montana. He had learned not to take those things too seriously.

One year when the big night came for the Indian Days Rodeo. Scott and Hank took 30 patients to the event with a barbeque picnic to follow. This evening went from bad to worse. The "rodeo" consisted mainly of Indian horse racing and Native American dancing. Each tribe dressed in traditional costumes and performed the dances of their ancestors. After several hours, Scott knew the constant beating of the tom-toms would stick in his head for months. The rodeo itself had started 45 minutes late because officials were unable to find the Master of Ceremonies. Scott was faced with 30 angry and hungry veterans. The plan was to attend the rodeo for a short while and then adjourn for a barbeque dinner. The veterans were definitely more interested in food than the Native American cultural activities. After a seemingly unbearably long time spent between keeping watch over and consoling the patients, the MC was discovered asleep under the stands, the victim of too much "firewater." The show could finally begin. By the time the races and dancing were over, the patients were starving, so Hank and Scott herded their charges over to the barbeque area. The main course consisted of wild game that had been donated by Sheridan area residents.

People in Wyoming are great hunters and often end up with more wild game in their freezers than the family and neighbors can consume. The local rodeo became a good place to dispose of excess meat without actually throwing it away. To conservative westerners, that would be just plain wasteful. Some of the donated fare was almost certainly over aged and freezer burned by the time it was used. The next day Scott was in major trouble with Medical Center nurses who had spent much of the night taking care of sick patients who had eaten that "aged" meat.

During the 1970's and 1980's, an Inter-Tribal Alcohol Treatment Center (ITATC) was co-located at the Sheridan VA Center.

Former Inter-Tribal Alcohol Treatment Center (ITATC)

The program was family oriented, with entire families living at the facility. Structured classes on alcohol treatment for patients and their families were offered with excellent instructors. The recreation therapy staff worked with the ITATC instructors to set up activities which involved both veteran patients and ITATC participants. These activities included horseshoe tournaments, volleyball games, and bowling. The VA had a bowling alley which had manual pin setters. During the 1960's and 1970's, the Native Americans would set pins for 10 cents a line. They had a bowling team in the VA league and a fierce but friendly rivalry developed between ITATC and veterans' teams. On one occasion the pin setters who, of course, were biased toward the Native American team found a way to string a metal wire across the lane in front of the pins. When the first veteran threw his ball down thc lanc it hit that wire and bounced across two adjoining lanes. At first, the veterans didn't realize what was happening, but it soon became obvious that there was no way they were going to score against the opposing team that night. Scott would never forget the laughter that resounded in that bowling alley as ball after ball bounced off that wire.

Bowling Alley

ITATC also had a softball team in the city softball league which was played at the VA facility. The two worst teams in the league were the veterans and the ITATC players. On the other hand, no other teams had as much fun playing each other as these two did and it became a great and friendly rivalry. Scott remembered all the good natured pranks and great times that occurred whenever the two teams met.

Although neither group really realized some of the things they had in common, Scott and the other therapists often discussed the similarities between the Sheridan veterans and the local Native American community. Both were highly dependent on the government for many of their daily needs. Like the veterans, the Native Americans had high incidences of alcoholism and mental disorders. Both groups were subject to the whims of government bureaucrats determined to cut expenses to minimize the cost of programs that were essential to the well-being of these citizens. Though for different reasons, neither group had asked to be put into this environment where every aspect of their lives was subject to government regulations and where something given could just as easily be taken away. In another sense, both the Sheridan veterans at the Medical Center and the Native Americans on the reservations were the unwanted step-children of a society that would just as soon forget they even existed.

Chapter 6

Like most government agencies, the Veteran's Administration is faced with difficult choices as the funding for veteran's services is subject to constant pressure both from within the federal administration and from the Congress. The need to reduce costs while maintaining critical services is a daily focus by the managers of the Veterans Affairs Department at all levels. At the same time, costs of services, particularly in the medical field are increasing at a pace that far exceeds the ability to keep up. This continuing situation has put many programs in areas such as recreational therapy at risk. In fact, at the Sheridan Medical Center, as in other locations, many of the recreational programs instituted by Scott, Hank and the others have been cut back or discontinued. As in other agencies, programs are subject to cuts and elimination when administration policies turn to decentralization or outsourcing of services as a cure-all for funds limitations.

Recreation therapy programs by their nature are cost effective only when they can service a large number of patients. In recent years, alternative approaches to providing medical and related services to veterans have supplanted some of the more long-established programs. Traditionally in Veterans Affairs (VA) medical centers, as in many other medical centers, health services had been divided among several professional disciplines, each headed by a chief. Clinical activity is coordinated through a committee of chiefs and a matrix organizational structure. This discipline-based "stovepipe" organization can be prone to several problems. The reporting structure can be complex. Reorganization, redeployment, and coordination of services can be difficult when multiple lines of authority exist. Workload expectations can be inconsistent. However, the traditional organization works well in one respect. Dedicated employees in ancillary medical support areas such as recreational therapy are granted more flexibility to develop innovative programs unconstrained by the more rigid direct medical care disciplines.

In the decade of the 1990's, in the name of efficiency, a number of alternative organizational approaches were introduced. These health service line or product line structures were defined as "a comprehensive set of services to meet the needs of a particular segment of the market ... or an integrated set of services ... distinguished from other services provided by the technologists or specialty employees such as recreation therapists." A key characteristic of a health service or "product" line approach is organization around integrated services or patient care functions. For example, all disciplines and staff involved in cardiology or in mental health are brought together in a single organizational structure. While this often works well for direct medical services, the VA's recreation therapy programs often were relegated to secondary importance as the recreation staff members were integrated into programs where recreational efforts were considered outside of the medical mainstream.

The product line organization is touted as a more efficient approach than the traditional discipline-based organization. As an example; from 1993 to 1997, the number of veterans served by one medical center increased by 21.1 percent. However, at the same time, use of in-patient services was reduced by more than 60 percent. Concurrently, the health care staff decreased by nearly 14 percent. At the same time, across VA medical centers nationwide, the length of in-facility stay for health treatment decreased 11 percent. Inpatient beds per 10,000 veterans decreased 31.2 percent nationwide. The percentage of resources dedicated to inpatient mental health care, for example, at VA centers nationwide as a percentage of total mental health resources decreased 11.2 percent.[1] This reduction of in-patient care services was due to the transition, seen at all hospitals in the country, to greater emphasis on treating significantly more illnesses using out-patient care methods. At the same time, the VA, mirroring the private sector medical establishment, was developing dramatically greater dependence on smaller, more numerous local, out-patient clinics as a way of treating greater numbers of veterans particularly in small towns or rural arcas.

To Scott and his fellow therapists, these changes were a mixed blessing. While recognizing some of the organizational benefits of the product line structure, they have come to realize that the hospital-based recreation programs they had built over several decades were gradually fading away on the tide of efficiency. As they observed these changes toward the end of their careers, they could not help but wonder the ultimate effect of the

---

[1] Mark S. Bauer, M.D., Thomas McGreevy, M.S.W. and Jeannette Chirico-Post, M.D., "Establishing a Function-Based Mental Health Service Line in a VA Medical Center," American Psychiatric Association, Vol. 51, No. 10, October 2000, p. 1307.

loss of these programs on the core of physically and mentally disabled veterans resident in the Medical Centers. As times and programs change, the VA recreation program must adapt to survive. One innovation that has occurred in the last two decades is the establishment of a series of larger-scale recreational events that can bring together greater numbers of veterans who continue to have special needs over and above direct medical care. Today, the VA sponsors a number of special events as part of recreation therapy. In 2007, these events included:

Winter Sports Clinic: April 1-6, Snowmass, Colo.
Wheelchair Games: June 19-23, Milwaukee, Wis.
Golden Age Games: Aug. 27-31, Houston, Texas
Creative Arts Festival: Oct. 22-28, St. Louis, Mo.

The Winter Sports Clinic provides disabled veterans with opportunities for self-development and personal challenge through participation in cold weather sports and leisure activities. In 2006, more than 70 newly injured military personnel from Operation Iraqi Freedom and Operation Enduring Freedom participated – many for the first time. At the Clinic, all participants are able to develop winter sports skills and take part in a variety of adaptive workshops, which help demonstrate that having a physical or visual disability need not be an obstacle to an active, rewarding life.

The VA has also come to recognize the value of partnering with private sector groups in sponsoring these recreational programs. In the case of the Winter Sports Clinic, the VA's partner is the Disabled American Veterans (DAV) organization. DAV is a non-profit, congressionally chartered, veteran's service organization. With more than 1.2 million members, DAV is an organization of disabled veterans who are focused on building better lives for disabled veterans and their families. The organization accomplishes this goal by providing free assistance to veterans in obtaining benefits and services earned through their military service. It is fully funded through its membership dues and public contributions. It is not a government agency and receives no government funds.

On April 2, 2007, Veterans Affairs Secretary R. James Nicholson opened the National Disabled Veterans Winter Sports Clinic, offering special thanks to wounded warriors of Iraq and Afghanistan and encouraging them to seize the opportunities that await them here. "There is controversy about this war, but there is no controversy about you," Nicholson told about 100 veterans of operations Iraqi Freedom and Enduring Freedom, who joined more than 350 other disabled veterans for this year's clinic.[2] Bradley Barton, national commander of the Disabled American Veterans, which cosponsors the clinic with the Department of Veterans Affairs, joined Nicholson in encouraging the country's newest disabled veterans to look beyond their limitations. Barton, who was paralyzed from the waist down during combat in Vietnam, told the group he's had almost 40 years to face his disability and find a way to succeed in life. "And to be very honest with you, after having gone through the process of adjusting to life with a disability, it is difficult to see your young men and women returning from another war with scars and wounds and the challenges that injuries bring." Barton said the winter sports clinic, made possible by generous corporate sponsors and an army of volunteers, gives him hope that the country is

---

[2] Ibid.

moving in the right direction in how it treats its disabled veterans. [3]

The VA Winter Sports Clinic had modest beginnings. In the winter of 1987, a recreational therapist from the Grand Junction Veterans Medical Center took a small group of disabled veterans to the local Powderhorn Ski Resort. This resort is located in the beautiful mountains of the Grand Mesa approximately 45 minutes from the city of Grand Junction, Colorado. The Grand Mesa is a giant island in the sky with an altitude of 10,000 feet. This mesa is the largest flat-top mountain in the world covering more than 230,000 acres and containing 300 lakes. These disabled veterans were able to spend the day skiing with the assistance of volunteers and the recreation staff. The recreation specialist from Grand Junction had no idea that this activity would eventually skyrocket into a national sports clinic with disabled veterans from every state in attendance. From this small beginning, it became evident that along with the physical benefits, the veterans grew in their feelings of self-worth, self-confidence, willingness to take chances, recognition and most of all, independence.

Participation in the VA special events is open to U.S. military service veterans with spinal cord injuries, orthopedic amputations, visual impairments, certain neurological problems and other disabilities. Veterans who are receiving health care at a Department of Veterans Affairs (VA) medical facility have first priority. In addition, a number of active duty military personnel from Operation Iraqi Freedom and Operation Enduring

---

[3] Referenced at:
http://www.defenselink.mil/news/newsarticle.aspx?id=32666

Freedom have attended in recent years to lend support to their comrades. More than 200 certified ski instructors for the disabled, and several current and former members of the U.S. Disabled Ski Team, serve as ski instructors. The program has developed to the point that a racing training and development program is held to help veterans develop their skiing abilities to an elite level, with an ultimate goal of qualifying for the U.S. Paralympic Team. In 2007, more than 450 participants from across the country attended the Clinic. Because of the success of the Winter Sports Clinic, the event grew from its original 10 veterans in 1987 to the 450 participants in 2007. Because of this remarkable growth, the event eventually moved from the Powderhorn Resort to the larger Snowmass Village resort near Aspen, Colorado.

In the first few years after its beginning, Hank started taking patients to the Sports Clinic in Grand Junction. Being a disabled vet himself, he had a place in his heart for these special veterans and always considered the Winter Sports Clinic as his "Super Bowl" of recreation therapy. The recreation staff was always impressed by Hank's level of enthusiasm when he returned to the VA after attending the sports clinic. Each year, Hank bussed the veterans the 10 hour drive from Sheridan to Snowmass Village. In the early years, he worked with amputee vets in the Nordic skiing program. Because of his extensive athletic training and experience in working with various disabilities he was able to be a key coach in many of the activities available to the participants including: adaptive skiing with mono-skis and bi-skis; instruction in adaptive Alpine (downhill) and Nordic (cross-country) skiing for stand-up skiers, including the visually impaired; alternate activities including scuba diving, sled hockey, snowshoeing, snowmobiling, rock climbing, trap shooting, fencing, golf, Snow Cat/Gondola Rides and a trip to the nearby Hot Springs; plus educational and instructional workshops on self-defense and other stimulating topics. He couldn't wait to tell Scott about the time that one of his responsibilities at the sports clinic was as movie star, Bo Derek's body guard. Scott's face lit up and he said, "What tough duty that must have been!" Ms. Derek was the National Chairperson for the clinic in 2005. Hank said that unlike some other celebrity volunteers, she really cared about the vets and actually worked hard for them. One of her responsibilities was to present the awards to the participants. Imagine what a thrill it was to receive an award from Bo Derek (A Perfect 10)!

Scott became very interested in the Winter Sports Clinic and he wanted to volunteer his skills. He asked Hank to describe the clinic in more detail at the monthly recreation meeting of the recreation staff. Hank explained to the staff that the Winter Sports Clinic is open to every veteran from World War I, World War II, the Korean Conflict, the Vietnam War, the Gulf War and the current conflicts in Iraq and Afghanistan. Any veteran with severe impairments or other qualifying disability may participate in the Winter Sports Clinic.

After its inception in 1987, the Department of Veteran Affairs had made a commitment to promote the sports clinic to help disabled veterans recover from their serious injuries and illnesses. In his talk, Hank described the multitude of activities that are available for these vets. Countless hours of planning have enabled the great people of Snowmass Village and the surrounding area to put together a special package to bring veterans from Walter Reed Hospital and other VA sites to Snowmass Village for the Winter Sports Clinic. Countless numbers of volunteers from local towns in the area come to Aspen each year to contribute to the success of the program. The Winter Sports Clinic shows the disabled veteran that his or her life can be changed forever. The veterans are always amazed at their success in meeting challenges they may have believed they could never overcome. No matter what branch of the service or what conflict they may have been in, the participants at the event form a strong bond through teamwork and competition.

At one introductory session, Hank was talking to a veteran from Denver, Colorado, who had lost both legs in a roadside bombing in Iraq. He was describing the clinic activities, and the veteran, with tears in his eyes said, "I can't believe these people would do this for me."

There were many similar stories. Hank spoke of the time he was working with a visually impaired Marine Corps veteran who had lost his sight in Vietnam. They were working on downhill skiing with a harness and a rope. The Marine told Hank that in his wildest dreams he never thought he could ski again. This story reminded Scott of the training program he had visited in Phoenix with blind bowlers. They had put rails on the alleys to guide the ball. Scott was amazed at the bowling scores these men and women were able to produce. Scott said that it put his bowling game to shame.

At another session Hank described an incredibly rewarding feeling he had received as he watched a vet from California, who was a double amputee, scuba dive for the first time. He would always remember the excitement of the moment they had shared. Hank, being a long-time horseman from Wyoming, was able to share his skills with a vet who had lost a leg in Iraq. The vet was from New York City and had never been on a horse! He had also received so much satisfaction from the Navy vet from Florida who went rock climbing for the first time and told Hank how much confidence he had gained from the experience. What an awesome sight it had been for Hank to see the double amputees playing sled hockey with all the hilarity that accompanied that activity. Sledge or sled hockey, as it's known in the U.S., is a sport that was designed to allow participants who have a physical disability to play the game of ice hockey. Ice sled hockey was invented in the early 1960s in Stockholm, Sweden at a rehabilitation center. It is currently one of the most popular sports in the Paralympics Games. The 2006 Paralympics Games in Torino, Italy, saw the gold medal go to Canada, silver to Norway and bronze to the United States. One particular story that always stayed with Hank was of the vet who had received a head wound in action near Baghdad. One year after coming so close to death, he attended his first Winter Sports Clinic. He said, "I didn't think I was going to be able to walk and one year later I was snowboarding."

A great aspect of the winter sports clinic is the tremendous difference in the ages of the vets. Older veterans are eager to share their insights with younger, more recently disabled vets. These younger vets learn that there truly are people who understand and care for them. In April of 2007, more than 450 disabled veterans arrived at Snowmass Village expecting a wonderful show. They were looking forward to participating in activities which were designed to push them to new heights. Previous experiences of both participants and volunteers have named what happens each year at Snowmass Village, "Miracles on the Mountainside." These courageous veterans demonstrate again and again that they refuse to let serious disabilities get in the way of a full and productive life. They form a special bond that keeps them coming back year after year.

The Winter Sports Clinic has demonstrated to thousands of disabled vets that even with a physical or visual disability one can still have a very rewarding life. One of Hank's concerns has been for the veterans who may never learn of the Winter Sports Clinic because of the changes that product-line and the advent of out-patient clinics have brought to recreation therapy programs throughout the VA system. While out-patient clinics may be a good thing for the veteran as far as travel expenses and other organizational efficiencies, he wonders how much of the real long-term benefits of recreation therapy treatment are being lost.[4]

---

[4] For information on eligibility and participation, or to be a volunteer, visit the website at http://www1.va.gov/vetevent/wsc/2007/Default.cfm

Chapter 7

By the spring of 2000, Scott was in his 30th year at the Sheridan VA Medical Center. Many changes had occurred in the way veterans were receiving health care services. Scott could see the benefits of some of these changes; however, the staff reductions and accompanying decline in recreational services available to hospitalized veterans became more and more discouraging to Scott and the entire recreation therapy staff. As his job became less fulfilling, Scott came to the realization that it was time for him to retire.

His last day at the V.A. Center was full of memories. This had been his 2nd home for over 30 years and many of his co-workers were like family. At his retirement ceremony, the chief of nursing presented him with a plaque commemorating his 30 years of dedicated service. He knew that his true reward came from the patients and those with whom he had worked so closely. After receiving the plaque and being congratulated by friends and co-workers, he headed to his office to collect his few personal belongings. But, before heading home, he began to reminisce about his memories of places and things that had occurred at the Center.

He decided to take one last walk around the facility and grounds. Scott visited the VA chapel one more time. He had such vivid memories of activities that had occurred here. In his mind he could see Chaplin Roberts and

Father Davenport presiding over weekly Protestant and Catholic services. He remembered the many memorial services he had attended over the last thirty years. Every one of those veterans who had passed on held a special meaning in Scott's heart. He hoped he had brought some comfort into their sometimes bleak lives.

During the early 1990's he had begun to attend the Promise Keepers Christian Men's Conferences. Their mission is to ignite and unite men to become passionate followers of Jesus Christ through the effective communication of their promise to devote themselves to God, their fellow men, family, church and the world. The Promise Keepers' vision is simply put in three words: "Men Transformed Worldwide." Based in Denver, Colorado, Promise Keepers has directly reached more than five and a half million men in conferences held since its founding in 1990.

After attending one such conference, Scott met a young patient from Denver. The man confided that he had been penniless and living on the streets near Mile High Stadium, home of the Denver Broncos professional football team. The man had heard the sound of men singing and began walking toward the sound. As he got nearer to the source of the music, he realized that it was "Amazing Grace" being sung by 50,000 men gathered in the stadium. These men were joined by a telecast of 80,000 men from Atlanta, Georgia. These thousands were also singing "Amazing Grace" on the big screen. The man had made his way to the stadium where he was ministered to by some of the Christian men at that gathering. Thanks to this demonstration of brotherly love, the man had renounced his old life and accepted Christ as his Savior. Some of his newfound friends had helped him go to the VA Hospital in Sheridan where he was admitted to the alcohol treatment unit. He completed the program and today is running a successful business.

This event led Scott to realize that there was a need for veteran patients to have the opportunity to learn more about a message of hope for their lives. He obtained permission from the administration to conduct voluntary Christian Bible studies at the Center. He felt that the Victory Over the Darkness video series by Neil Anderson would be a good starting point for such a study. This volunteer study was well attended and appreciated by the patients. Scott felt that it was one of the most rewarding activities he had accomplished during his time at the VA.

Next, Scott walked by the swimming pool. He remembered the time the Hospital Week Committee planned a staff dunking booth at the pool. Throughout the day, staff members from every department: medical doctors, nurses, psychiatrists, psychologists, administrators, and therapists were able to socialize without any thought of their professional position. The day's activities helped bring the whole staff together almost as a family. Everyone had such a great time that people were still talking about it.

One of the nurses, Jan Little, had been at the Center for 25 years. She was especially good with patients and treated each with the caring attention they deserved. Although only five feet four inches tall, Jan was a ball of fire. She was originally from New York City and her big city sense of humor had gotten her through tough situations over the years. She used any excuse to remind

Scott about one of those embarrassing life moments that had occurred the day of the dunking booth. The therapeutic swimming pool was built in the 1920s. It was about ten feet by twenty feet and five feet deep and had the old fashioned drainage gutter around the edge. As it was Scott's duty to supervise the dunking booth activity, he was in the pool leaning against the edge when he suddenly realized that his elbow was stuck in one of the drainage outlets. The more he pulled, the more his elbow began to swell and the more agitated he became. He could just see the fire department showing up to cut off some part of his arm to get it unstuck from the outlet. He didn't want to let anyone know that he was stuck, but he knew he needed help. He signaled for Hank to come to his aid, trying not to draw any attention to himself. Hank was six feet four inches tall and 250 pounds of muscle. His arms looked like tree trunks, but he was as tender as a weeping willow. Gently, he attempted to massage Scott's arm free from the drain's clutches, but these efforts failed and they began to draw attention from the dunking booth participants. As people gathered around, it seemed like each had a different idea of how to solve the situation. Finally, they decreased the swelling with cold water and applied Vaseline and his arm was freed. From then on, Jan took every opportunity to tell the story of the only person she knew who could get stuck to a swimming pool. Scott had to admit it seemed much funnier years later than it had been at the time.

Scott walked past the running track that was used for another favorite event, the mile and five mile Fun Runs organized by Lucy, his long-time therapist partner. He couldn't help but remember the smiling faces of the patients who had participated in the Fun Run each year.

Lucy had been such a dynamic therapist, always working hard to improve the recreation therapy program. He could still picture her cheering on each patient whether they were attempting the one mile walk, one mile run, the five mile walk, or the five mile run. The look on their faces as they received participation ribbons couldn't have been more gratifying if they had won an Olympic medal. The interactions of staff and patients during events such as these really helped build trusting relationships between staff and patients.

He continued past the auditorium. So many memories! Like the night the United Service Organization, USO, show came to the Center. Ten minutes before the show was to begin, his manager and Scott couldn't find George Jessel, the star of the show. Billed as the "Toast Master General of the United States," for his frequent role as master of ceremonies at political and entertainment gatherings. Jessel was famous for his good-natured wit aimed at his fellow celebrities. Unfortunately he had a fondness for alcohol. After searching everywhere they could think of on the V.A. grounds, his manager asked, "Where's the nearest bar?" They headed for the Golden Branch where they found Jessel sitting at the bar. His manager said, "What are you doing here?"

"I never go on stage without having a drink first," he replied. They quickly returned to the V.A., where Mr. Jessel and Scott went backstage to prepare for the show. Jessel's close friend, comedian Jack Benny, had died recently, and not knowing what else to say, Scott told him that he was sorry to hear about his friend, Jack. Jessel burst into tears just as the curtain was going up. Scott remembered thinking that he was going to be responsible for ruining the whole event. But, being the showman that he was, Jessel pulled himself together and presented a tremendously entertaining show - much to Scott's relief.

The VA Center's multipurpose sports complex included a softball field, two tennis courts, two horseshoe pits, a basketball court, and a soccer field. The complex was surrounded by mature cottonwood trees overlooked by the beautiful snowcapped Big Horn Mountains. The sports field was perfectly landscaped and maintained by the Veterans Administration grounds crew.

Sports Field

Many of the sports activities were played under the big sky evenings with the sunset disappearing over the west end of the field. The evenings turned into a million stars over the entire Big Sky country. As Scott stood at home plate on the softball field for the last time, he remembered one of the few victories that his patient softball team had won over four years of city league play. He couldn't recall the team they were playing or the exact circumstance of the win. But, he could remember watching as men of many different backgrounds and professions celebrated together - cheering, hugging one another and congratulating each other. Any kind of win for these patients was considered a major victory. He remembered his feeling of pride at being able to provide such a positive experience for these alcohol and psychiatric patients. This memory made him happy that the tradition of dousing the coach with a bucket of cold water had not yet been established among the veterans.

Memories flooded his mind as he drove off of the V.A. grounds for the last time. Fort Road, as the entrance of Fort MacKenzie had been called for over a hundred years, was impeccably landscaped. As he left the V.A. property he could see the majestic Big Horn Mountains in the background and on each side of the rolling hills over which the road flowed, beautiful evergreen and deciduous trees had been planted.

American Buffalo (Bison) and Big Horn Mountains

The occasional sighting of an elk or a buffalo was always a thrill. In his mind's eye he could see all of the colors of the changing seasons; the bright red, vivid gold, and deep

orange of fall, the peaceful white cover of winter, and all of the shades of green in spring and summer.
So many times staff and patients had been struck by the spectacular beauty of sunsets over the Big Horns as they returned to the hospital grounds at the end of a recreational outing. Driving down that lane for the final time, he recalled barely missing a bobcat that had bounded across the road in front of his car and seeing the white tail deer that frequented the grounds and could jump those tall fences from a complete stand still. He remembered the pheasants as well as the wild turkeys patiently awaiting his arrival so that they could chase his car to the gate. Overseeing everything were the ever vigilant barn owls that resided in the towering cottonwoods.

Scott thought of how far the V.A. hospital system had come from the "guards at the gate" to the present "open campus" policy. He reminisced about the thousands of patients that had left the hospital with dreams of a better life, but he also had sorrowful memories of veterans who had died at the facility over his thirty year tenure, some with no friends or family and only the staff to comfort them in their final moments. He thought of fellow staff members and friends who had been shot, shot at, and in several cases, murdered by out-of-control veteran patients.

He traveled into Sheridan past the quaint junior college in its lovely setting at the foot of the mountains. He had attended hundreds of basketball games with the patients in its golden domed auditorium. He distinctly recalled the night that Lucy had taken her first trip with patients to a Sheridan College basketball game. During the most thrilling part of the fourth quarter, Milo Thurston, a geriatric patient suddenly collapsed onto the court from the front row of the stands. Lucy didn't know if he was suffering a heart attack or not so she called the local 911 emergency number and then went to help Milo. When he saw her kneeling over him, Milo's first question was, "Where are my teeth?" Lucy was not aware of the VA policy which was to call the VA medical staff that would transport a sick or disabled patient back to the VA. The city 911 emergency response staff instead transported Milo to Sheridan Memorial Hospital. The Center's Chief Medical Accountant about choked when he saw the bill. Needless to say the recreation staff never again forgot that policy!

Next, Scott drove past Kendrick Park where he and Kate had walked together on many warm, tranquil evenings.

Kendrick Park and Bandstand

Kendrick Park is a beautiful municipal park near the center of the Sheridan with mature cottonwoods, playgrounds for the children, tennis courts, a swimming pool, and the bandstand situated at the base of the buffalo and elk pasture. During mating season a person could listen to the bugling of the majestic bull elk as they called for their mates. The park bandstand was a perfect setting for summer band concerts. There was music from a different genre each week, but no matter the type of music, the patients always found peace and tranquility while attending the concerts.

That peace was shattered one evening when a veteran needed to use the facilities. Scott directed him to the nearest restroom which happened to be in the men's locker room at the swimming pool. When he hadn't returned after a short period, Scott became concerned and went to look for him. He arrived at the pool just in time to see the patient do a swan dive from the high board - fully clothed. Panicked children exited the pool as if they were swimming for their lives from a great white shark. Scott had to return the patient to the hospital while Kate, who had volunteered to help that evening, remained at the park to supervise the remaining patients. From that point on, Scott was known to many as the V.A. Aquatics Director.

Viewing the Big Horns from the park that day, cause him to think of those picnics on which he had taken the patients for many years. They loved the Big Horn Mountains because Pine Island, their picnicking area, had lakes and a river surrounded by gorgeous scenery as well as wildlife such as buffalo, moose, deer and elk. Being in the park also reminded Scott of the great finale to his career. The recreation staff had orchestrated a gag-filled retirement party which had been held at the Kendrick Park bandstand. There was music, great food and entertainment. As Scott looked back on this event, most of the entertainment seemed to have been centered on the many blunders that he had made through the years. He had been touched by the number of people who came to share stories and memories from the last thirty years, and knew that he was going to miss these people who had become part of his extended family.

As Scott approached his retirement from the VA, he had experienced many feelings. The majority of these were positive. He thought of all of the recreation programs that Hank, Lucy and he had started throughout their careers. He also thought of the many lives that they hopefully had touched and perhaps even changed. Over the years they always attempted to put the needs of veterans first, and knew that they had accomplished that goal to the best of their abilities. His thoughts were also with the staff members that had become a part of his life. He had acquired wonderful friendships which would last a lifetime.

Epilogue

Most Americans believe that a veteran is a person who serves his country in the military and then comes home and goes back to his previous life including family, friends and job. This book was written to help develop an awareness of the thousands of veterans who, because of their wartime experiences, are unable to return to life as they knew it before their military service. These are the forgotten veterans.

The need to go to war is always controversial. Unfortunately, many people fail to differentiate between our natural aversion for war itself and the desire to fully support those men and women who are willing to serve. In the years since the Second World War, America has been involved in many conflicts around the globe. None of these were "declared wars" and some were not supported by a significant part of the population. It is essential, however, that we distinguish between our feelings for or against a particular military action and our support of those who are called on to leave our shores and be part of the conflict.

Why does it matter? Our service men and women are willing to make the ultimate sacrifice for the people and the country that they love. No one ever entered the military service with expectations of riches or an easy life. However, when young people enlist in our Armed Forces, they are promised a number of benefits upon completion of their service times. These include furthering their education, medical care, home loans and ultimately, respectful burial services. Unfortunately, since the very beginning of our country, the sanctity of promises to returning veterans has, on many occasions, been diminished in the face of political agendas and budgetary deficits. As we have seen in the stories recalled in this book, the needs of the veterans returning home are as basic as merely having a place to live or minimal medical care to treat the long-term effects of the ravages of combat. All Americans need to remember the sacrifices of these sometimes forgotten heroes and keep the promises made to these men and women when they agreed to serve our country. Today a memorial stands on the grounds of the Sheridan VA Medical Center to honor those veterans who have been treated at this facility.

Where do we go from here? Like most organizations in government, the Veteran's Administration is today under great pressure to reduce costs and build greater efficiencies into the veteran's medical and benefits system. The VA operates the nation's largest integrated health care system with more than 1,400 sites of care, including hospitals, community clinics, nursing homes, domiciliaries, readjustment counseling centers, and various other facilities employing 14,800 doctors and 61,000 nurses. By policy, the VA is attempting to transition from large facilities providing long term care to severely impacted patients to smaller, more numerous activities, capable of administering to increasing numbers of medically challenged veterans coming home from the Nation's world-wide security commitments.

The number of returning Iraq and Afghanistan combat veterans visiting Department of Veterans' Affairs walk-in clinics has more than doubled since 2004, while the clinics' staff has increased by less than 10%, agency records show. These clinics, known as Vet Centers, are meant to make it easier for combat veterans to receive help. In 2006, 21,681 Iraq and Afghanistan veterans visited the centers, up from 8,965 in 2004. The Vet Centers are small, storefront operations with a staff of four to five people each. The centers were created in 1979 to help Vietnam War veterans readjust to society. Services include combat stress counseling, marriage therapy, job assistance and medical referrals.

Changing approaches to medical care such as the VA outpatient clinics appear to be quite efficient when it comes to saving travel time to and from hospital stays and seeing greater numbers of patients. However, the standard of care often decreases at these clinics compared to the services that are available in the more traditional inpatient facility. Services such as therapeutic recreation, educational therapy, occupational therapy, and other aspects of rehabilitation therapy require a longer-term horizon to effectively treat many chronic conditions common to some returning veterans. These treatments have proven to have lasting benefits for the whole person rather than simply addressing the immediate medical issues a veteran might be facing. Yet, most of us are blissfully unaware of the changes that are occurring in the VA medical system. In 2006, the Administration proposed cutting $47 million from the $3.3 billion budget for veterans' readjustment benefits. Two congressional committees agreed, but Congress didn't pass a final spending bill. In 2007, Congress passed a resolution that keeps spending at the 2006 levels.[5] It is not clear what direction future administrations and the Congress will take in supporting the VA medical care program.

By documenting in a small way the real-life stories of a few of the veterans who continue to require more personalized care over longer periods, this book attempts, through a mixture of humor, sadness and some real-life drama, to keep alive the vision and the promises made to our veterans across the years of our history. Despite the theatrics and athletic prowess we see daily on our TV and motion picture screens, the veterans are the "real" American heroes. We can thank them for defending and preserving our American "way of life." Let's never let them be forgotten.

---

[5] Zoroya, Gregg, "Staffing at Vet Centers Lagging, USA TODAY, April 19, 2007.